For Bigfoot and things that go bump in the night.

Thank you to Hayley Stevens for her occult expertise.

Tremendous gratitude to the Flying Eye elves
for their wisdom and hard work.

Also in the series:

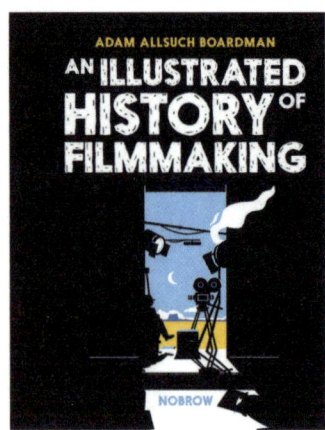 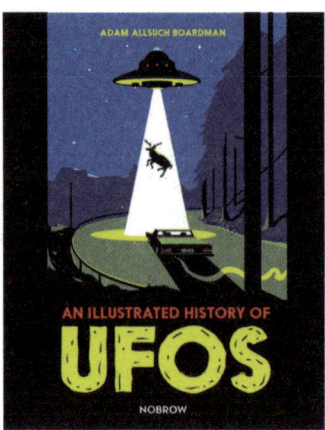 

First edition published in 2024 by Flying Eye Books Ltd.
27 Westgate Street, London, E8 3RL.

Text and illustrations © Adam Allsuch Boardman 2024

Consultant: Hayley Stevens

Adam Allsuch Boardman has asserted his right under the Copyright, Designs
and Patents Act, 1988, to be identified as the Author and Illustrator of this Work.

All rights reserved. No part of this publication may be reproduced or transmitted in any form or
by any means, electronic or mechanical, including photocopying, recording or by any information
and storage retrieval system, without prior written consent from the publisher.

Edited by Kate Birch and Christina Webb
Designed by Sarah Crookes

1 3 5 7 9 10 8 6 4 2

Published in the USA by Flying Eye Books Ltd.
Printed in Poland on FSC® certified paper.

ISBN: 978-1-83874-168-6
www.flyingeyebooks.com

ADAM ALLSUCH BOARDMAN

AN ILLUSTRATED HISTORY OF
URBAN LEGENDS

FLYING EYE BOOKS

CONTENTS

The Chupacabra, as reported in Puerto Rico, circa 1995

Introduction 8
What is an Urban Legend?
Skeptical Inquiry
The Spread of Urban Legends

Premodernity 16
Aquatic Anomalies
Odd Dogs
Lost Cities
Vampires
Ghosts
Little Lights

Modernity 30
Salacious Sprees
Checked Out
Tremendous Trees
Worse Has Happened at Sea
Hollow Earth
Wartime Legends
Mysterious Disappearances

Midcentury 42
Cryptozoology
Yeti
Road Rumours
UFOs
Odd Attractions
Media Legends
Phenomena
Freaky Fatalities
Bigfoot
Space Stories
Mothman

The Postmodern Era 66
Home Invaders
Creepy Contamination
Gallery of Cryptids
You Had to Be There
The Stranger
Xeroxlore
Animal Antics
Going Underground
Work of the Devil
Strange Places
Terrible Technology
Objects Associated With Legends

Metamodern Era 92
Videogames
Screen Legends
Send in the Clowns
Far-flung Travellers
Sweet Dreams
Legendary Rogues Gallery
TV Debunkery
Internet Invention
Rituals
Phantom Places
Urban Legends in Media
Cryptid Photos

Urban Legends Today 114
(Real) People of Urban Legends 116
Glossary 118
Further Reading 120
Further Viewing 122
Index 124

INTRODUCTION

Most people know of the legendary Bigfoot or the rumoured alligators lurking in New York's sewers, but have you heard the one about the photocopier that predicts your fate?

From the campfire to the digital rumour mill, urban legends have flourished wherever we tell stories. Despite dubious credibility, these stories manage to spread across continents and generations. Urban legends range from mundane hazards of microwaves and baths to the paranormal pantheon of vanishing hitchhikers and giant moth men.

Whether once true, sprouted from half remembered facts or entirely fictional, we have scrutinised these legends for centuries. Today, we speculate on the meanings of popular tales, all the while new mutations spawn with ever familiar themes and scenarios.

Contained within these pages are tales older than time, unsolved mysteries and stories stranger than fiction. This book will ferry you across a river of uncanny tales, from classic folklore to contemporary urban legend. So, check the closet, make sure the skies are clear and delve in if you are ready to imagine the strange.

The JATO Rocket Car, circa 1990s.

WHAT IS AN URBAN LEGEND?

American academic and folklorist Richard Dorson first coined the term 'urban legend' in the 1950s. He described them as folktales told in modern cities. Over time, this meaning has grown to become a mysterious, humorous or horrific story circulated as truth. In most cases these stories are found to be made up or exaggerated.

Legend
Legends are stories about people and places that may or may not be authentic but are often believed by an audience.

Myth
Myths are stories tied strongly to a belief system, such as the Bible or ancient Greek myths. Myths can take thousands of years to develop and are often used to explain mysterious phenomena.

Types of Stories
Writers group urban legends into categories based on the content of the stories. Below are several common themes:

Contamination
Alarmist paranoia about everyday products.

Animals
Amusing or horrid incidents with animals.

Bogeymen
Terrifying accounts of murderers and monsters.

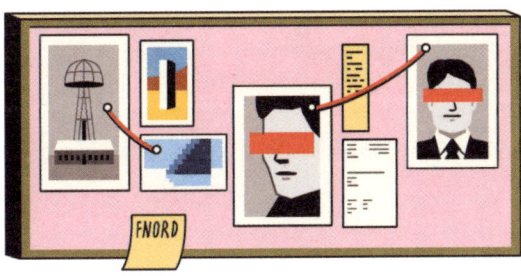

Conspiracies
Mysterious plots and schemes.

Paranormal
Alleged encounters with the unknown.

Technology
Frustrations and misconceptions about common technology.

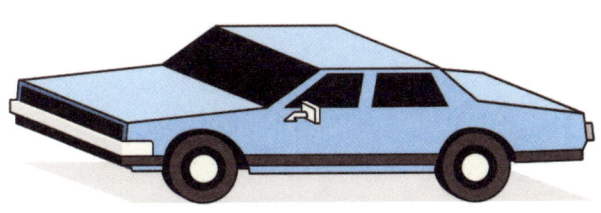

Road Rumours
Strange happenings in and around cars.

SKEPTICAL INQUIRY

When urban legends are studied in detail, rather than accepted on faith, it is called 'skeptical inquiry'. Skeptics can range from academics to amateur enthusiasts, and their agenda can range from scrutinising the origins of stories to forging their own retellings.

Skeptic
A good skeptic uses evidence-based inquiry to discover the truth.

Ghost Hunter
A specialist in the study of alleged hauntings.

Cryptozoologist
A person who studies legendary animals whose existence is disputed.

Ufologist
Someone who specialises in the study of unidentified flying objects.

Folklorist
Academics and writers with a literary interest in urban legends. They collect, compare and analyse stories.

Journalist
Journalists are regularly tasked with distinguishing urban legends from genuine news.

Entertainers
Some writers, TV presenters and content creators speculate upon urban legends.

Most urban legends are harmless and amusing, however there are several things to consider when researching an urban legend:

Slander and Libel
Some legends are spread deliberately to defame a company or person.

Purpose
Urban legends often convey a social meaning. For example, it could be a caution about everyday dangers.

Authorship
It is sometimes possible to prove that a story has been made up by someone.

Age
Urban legends may have been in circulation for centuries, with changes to details.

Entertainment
Storytellers often play up the comedy or horror of stories to entertain their audience. For instance, there is a 1960s tale about a contractor who poured cement over a car, thinking it belonged to his wife's secret lover. Allegedly, it turned out his wife had bought the car as a gift to the contractor.

THE SPREAD OF URBAN LEGENDS

Historically, urban legends were passed orally from person to person, as a genre of folklore. Then, in the 19th century, a growing number of folklorists began to seek out these stories, keen to document legends from around the world. Since then, new technologies have allowed urban legends to spread faster than ever before.

Oral Tradition
Originally, urban legends were passed by word-of-mouth. Stories have been told everywhere, from the glow of campfires to the comfort of our homes.

Publishing
As more people became literate in the 19th century, writers began documenting folklore from around the world, including the famous German academics, *The Brothers Grimm*. Books, newspapers and journals have all helped spread urban legends.

News
The many incarnations of news media share urban legends on a regular basis. Reportage may show a skeptic and supportive opinions about the stories. Some outlets have been known to lean into sensationalist tales to attract an audience.

Xeroxlore

Xeroxlore, or copylore, are urban legends shared on posters and fliers. These self-published works were a precursor to the content that is seen on the internet today. Xeroxlore may still be found cluttering noticeboards and walls.

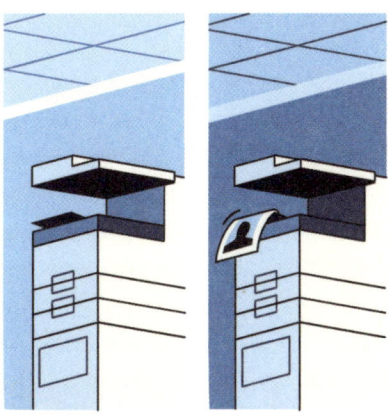

Radio and Podcasts

Late-night radio show *Coast to Coast AM* is best known for broadcasting live calls about UFOs, ghosts and urban legends. Since the mid-2000s, thousands of paranormal-themed podcasts have brought urban legends to numerous ears.

Social Media

Today, anyone with internet access can use social media to spread legends quickly. There is a great responsibility for the user to think critically about the context, intent and source of stories found online more than ever before.

Ostension

Ostension is a message sent through the miming of actions, such as pointing to mean 'that way'. Folklorists use the term to describe how people change their behaviour because of urban legends, from avoiding a house because it is said to be haunted to the extremes of mass hysteria.

PREMODERNITY

Possible depiction of the Loch Ness Monster, circa 12th century.

AQUATIC ANOMALIES

Rivers, lakes and springs have historically attracted human ritual, in the form of temples, offerings and stories. Local tales warn that waterways are inhabited by monsters and spirits. Folklorists often suggest the stories are parabolic, meant to deter youths from dangerous waters.

Loch Ness Monster

In legend, Loch Ness, Scotland has been home to an aquatic monster since at least the 6th century. In 1933, contemporary interest was sparked when *The Inverness Courier* reported a sighting by a holidaying couple. Nicknamed 'Nessie', the monster became the muse of hunters and tourists.

An Irregular Reptile

Many believe that the Loch Ness Monster is a *plesiosaur*, an ancient predatory reptile that went extinct with the dinosaurs around 65 million years ago. This hypothesis is not accepted by most experts in the natural sciences.

Fish, Elephants and Submarines

Alleged photos, sketches and films have regularly appeared in the press. Skeptics suggest a range of animals may have been mistaken for the monster, including circus elephants, otters, eels and big fish.

The 'Surgeon's Photograph' (1934), shared in newspapers in the 20th century, is easily the most famous alleged picture of the monster. In 1975, the *Sunday Telegraph* claimed the photo was hoaxed by sculpting a reptilian head onto a toy submarine.

Modified toy submarine

An elephant

Attack of the Globster

The giant corpse of a *con rit* (Vietnamese for centipede) was said to have washed up on a Vietnamese beach in 1833. Paranormal enthusiasts have labelled it a *globster*, which is a strange-looking decomposed animal. Skeptics say that most globsters are simply ordinary animals, decayed beyond recognition.

Lake Van Monster

Armenian folklore suggests the existence of a *vishap* (water dragon) in Lake Van, Turkey. In 1889, a newspaper reported that a man was dragged into the lake's depths by the beast. Skeptics believe sightings have been inspired by the Loch Ness Monster, promoted to attract tourism. Divers exploring the lake have not found any evidence of a large aquatic monster. However, divers in 2016 took intriguing photos of old castle walls submerged deep in the lake. Archaeologists suspect the ruins were built by castle builders in the Middle Ages.

It is thought the medieval builders reused masonry from 3000-year-old Urartian ruins, much of which is still visible above water.

ODD DOGS

Dogs, one of our oldest animal companions, are a common subject of urban legends. Though often characterised as faithful friends, these pages detail more unusual examples.

Beast of Gévaudan

In the late 18th century, a large wolf plagued communities in France. While carrying an aura of legend-making, the attacks were very real and attracted the attention of King Louis XV, who decreed for the animal's death. There are many accounts of nobles, soldiers and commoners alike tackling the beast. Local heroine Marie-Jeanne Valet was said to have speared a wolf in the stomach, leaving it critically injured.

The beast was finally felled by the hunter Jean Chastel. As per the traditional narrative, the remains were buried in the gardens of a private Parisian mansion. Scholars believe reports of the attacks were heightened by mass-hysteria, which led the French populace to imbue the beast with supernatural powers.

Some scholars have debated whether the beast could have been a hyena, lion or an Italian grey wolf.

Dog Lady Island

In Monroe, USA, a small island was once home to a mansion estate. Following a fire in 1961, it was believed a widowed woman remained, with only a pack of dogs for company. In local legend, the woman lost her tongue fighting with one of the dogs over a carcass. In other versions, she was killed by a gang of people and now haunts the island with a pack of Doberman Pinschers.

Jinmenken

The *Jinmenken* (Japanese for human-face dog) have featured in Japanese folklore since the 17th century. During the Edo period, supposed taxidermies and live specimens were exhibited at touring *misemono* (curio shows). During the 1980s, some were supposedly seen rifling through bins in Tokyo.

Werewolves

In folklore, werewolves are people who can shape-shift into wolves, typically under a full moon. In late medieval Europe, those believed to be werewolves were often trialled and punished in a similar manner to suspected witches.

Werewolves on Screen

Since the 20th century, cinema has had the greatest influence on the werewolf archetype, even popularising it in countries where wolves have long since been extinct. The on-screen werewolf has evolved from predominantly practical effects (an actor in costume) to the more widespread use of computer graphics.

The Wolfman (1941)   *Ginger Snaps (2000)*   *Bhediya (2022)*

LOST CITIES

Many stories about lost cities came from a colonialist age of exploration. Colonialists believed they were 'discovering' new lands, which inspired legends about undiscovered cities. In reality, these 'found' places belonged to natives. Sixteenth century European conquistadors searched for non-existent cities of gold (amongst more tangible plunders) in South America, but ended up causing devastating war and disease. Whilst the cities on these pages are likely fictional, there are examples of real lost cities. Most famously, the 15th century settlement of Machu Picchu was lost until explorers stumbled across it in the 19th century.

Atlantis

According to legend, Atlantis was a marvellous city cast to the depths of the ocean by a volcanic eruption. In reality, the 5th century BCE Greek writer, Plato, made up Atlantis to illustrate the dangers of pride and defiance of the gods. Plato may have based his tale on any number of cities sacked or ruined in ancient times.

Lost City of Ys

The city of Ys (pronounced eess) is rumoured to have once stood on the coast of Brittany, France and was built from gold, marble and valuable timbers. People believe it was lost when the king's daughter, Dahut, accidentally (or drunkenly) opened the city's sea defences and sunk the city. One day, the legend foretells, Ys will emerge from the depths.

El Dorado

From the 16th century, European conquistadors sought the remains of a legendary king of the Muisca people in South America. In time, the legend of *El Rey Dorado* ('The Golden King' in Spanish) broadened to El Dorado, a legendary golden city.

Lemuria

Twentieth century occultists and science fiction enthusiasts popularised the legend of Lemuria, a supposed lost civilisation in the Indian ocean. This legendary city was believed to have been populated by technologically advanced people with spaceships and telepathic powers. These familiar themes were influenced by the growing interest in flying saucers.

VAMPIRES

Popular culture has followed Western ideas about vampires since the 19th century. Familiar tropes and references to Vlad Dracula, a 15th century Romanian ruler, are thanks to Irish writer Bram Stoker's 1897 novel *Dracula*. Elsewhere, Malay cultures speak of the *Penanggalan*, a floating head that feasts on the blood of pregnant women, whilst the Betsileo people of Madagascar have Ramanga, a creature that sucks blood and eats nail clippings.

Vampire Deterrence in Folklore

Religious Iconography	Salt	Seeds	Dismemberment	Silver	Garlic

Empusa
In Greek stories, Empusa were creatures who drank blood and ate men. They were thought to have a leg made from metal (or sometimes a donkey's leg).

Jiangshi
Popularised in 18th century China, these hopping vampires were believed to drain victims' life force (known as *qi*).

Revenant
An animated corpse that haunts the living. In folklore the technical distinction between ghost, vampire and revenant is often unclear.

Psychological Warfare

In the 1950s, the United States helped the Philippine government combat armed rebels. Having studied the region's folklore, US specialists spread rumours about a vampiric demon called Aswang. The US military then drained a prisoner of their blood and left them dead in the open. Allegedly, this shocking act caused rebels to flee the area.

Dearg Due
A vampire woman said to be buried under a tree in Waterford, Ireland.

Carter Brothers
Vampiric siblings who were said to stalk around New Orleans, USA during the 1930s.

Don Jorge
Said to have hunted in Guadalajara, Mexico in the 19th century. A tree marks his supposed grave.

Count Orlak   Dracula   Edward Cullen

Vampires on Screen

In cinema, vampires remain predominately male, and range from the monstrous to the charming. Dracula's cape and tuxedo, popularised by Bela Lugosi's films, originated from theatre. Actor Raymond Huntley supposedly came up with the costume for his role in the 1924 *Dracula* production in the UK.

GHOSTS

Traditionally, ghosts are the spirits of the dead, often found lurking near places important to their former lives. They have featured in stories longer than we have written them down and they are an endless cause for speculation. Today, ghost hunters and skeptics visit haunted locations to find evidence for their existence or provide rational explanations.

Ghosts Around the World

La Llorona
Spanish for 'The Wailer'. If you follow her nightly wails a bad fate awaits you.

Bloody Mary
A ghost said to appear in mirrors around the world.

La Santa Compaña
A legendary procession of ghosts in Portugal and Spain.

Cherry the Ghost Dog
The supposed ghost of a beloved pet, witnessed in Finland.

Luz Mala
Spanish for 'Evil lights'. These sparkling orbs are said to float around in Argentina.

Poltergeist
A ghostly presence that makes itself known by moving objects.

Duppy
Ghost legends from the Caribbean and West Africa. There are different methods to keep each duppy at bay.

Lord Bothwell
Bothwell is said to haunt his former residence of Dragsholm Castle, Denmark.

Yūrei
Ghosts known in Japanese legends come in a variety of shapes and sizes.

Going Up

This legend began with a night shift nurse sharing a lift with a stranger. Before reaching their destination, the doors opened on the second floor. Alone in the hall stood a boy waiting to enter. The nurse jabbed the button to close the doors. Seeing the stranger's shocked expression, the woman explained, 'I saw that boy die two days ago, he was still wearing the red tag we attach to the deceased.' The man replied, 'Oh, like mine?' He too was a ghost! This story is particularly well known in the Philippines, but is common across Asia.

The Dead Travel Fast

In this tale, a woman was caught in a freezing downpour and hailed a taxi by a graveyard. Shivering in the back seat, she tapped the driver's shoulder to get their attention. The driver turned to reveal a shrieking, skeletal face. The woman was never heard from again. The story may have started in Argentina, but has versions in China and the USA.

LITTLE LIGHTS

Around the world there are said to be small lights that appear near paths. Skeptics believe they are caused by a range of phenomena, including luminescent insects and natural gasses.

Minmin Lights
Since the early 20th century, these fuzzy lights have been said to erratically follow cars in the Australian outback. For most drivers, the only hint of the phenomena are the number of road signs that advertise their presence.

Luz da Caniceira
The lights of Caniceira are an aerial phenomena seen in northern Portugal. The lights seemingly stalk travellers on lonely rural roads and can change colours. Traditionally, they are thought to be the ghost of a baby.

Luces del Tesoro
The Spanish phrase for 'treasure lights'. It is said these phantom illuminations lead to buried riches. The legends are best known in Central and South America.

Will-o'-the-Wisp
In British folklore, these lights are thought to be elemental beings (fairies and other nature spirits). In various British local legends, they are said to lure travellers from the road into dangerous marshes. The will-o'-the-wisps made a charming appearance in Disney's animated film, *Brave* (2012).

MODERNITY

Depiction of Spring-Heeled Jack in an English 'penny dreadful', circa 1860.

SALACIOUS SPREES

Some criminals' actions are so scandalous that they pass into the haze of urban legend. While there were likely culprits responsible for a number of crimes, newspapers and 'penny dreadfuls' (cheap periodicals) inflated their hype and spread mass hysteria.

The Wizard Bombardier
In the 1880s, citizens north of Melbourne, Australia came under attack by an individual known as the Wizard Bombardier. Wearing white robes and a sugar loaf hat (an archaic tall hat), the prankster screamed at passersby and pelted them with small rocks.

Ghost Hoaxers
Ever since the wake of 19th century interest in spirits, people dress as ghosts to frighten others. In 1877, one woman in Wagga, Australia hid in dark corners and scared people by dressing in a white outfit and a horrifying paper mask.

Spring-Heeled Jack
In the streets of 19th century England, a criminal harassed women and flummoxed men with acrobatic flair. The press dubbed him Spring-Heeled Jack for his daredevil antics on rooftops and signature leaping. Victims gave varying statements to the police about his appearance, ranging from a rake-thin gentleman to a fire-breathing devil.

The Mad Gasser
In 1944, citizens of Mattoon, USA reported an assault of noxious odours. According to victims, clouds of sickly fumes sneaked through windows, leaving people paralysed or sick. Various witnesses connected the gas with the appearance of a figure in black clothes. Hysteria led people to call the police at the first sniff of frightful fumes.

CHECKED OUT

Hotel legends tap into travel anxieties and everyday concerns, spreading strange tales of travellers and tourists alike.

Mum's the Word
This British legend from 1889 began with a woman leaving her sickly mother in a Parisian hotel while she looked for medicine. Upon her return, she found no trace of the room or her mother, and none of the hotel staff remembered her mother's arrival. Some versions reveal the mother died of the black plague and the hotel staff covered it up so as not to deter tourists. Elements of this story have appeared in mystery thrillers, such as Ethel Lina White's novel *The Wheel Spins* (1936) and the Jodie Foster film *Flightplan* (2005).

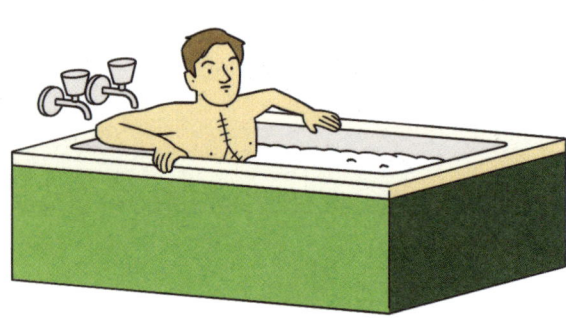 

Vital Organs
In the late 1990s, chain emails circulated warning travellers that hotels (usually in Las Vegas or New Orleans) were rife with organ thieves. According to the story, victims would wake in their hotel room bath filled with ice and realise that their kidneys had been removed overnight. It's possible the story was inspired by a black market organ sale that took place in Berlin in 1991.

The Good Book
The Evangelical Christian group known as Gideons stocked many American hotel rooms with a free Bible. As early as the 1990s, a rumour spread that the group were slipping $100 bills into the bibles for dedicated readers.

TREMENDOUS TREES

Objects with any sort of permanence are likely enough to gain a legend or two if they hang around long enough. Trees that live for decades and centuries often become the subject of tales whilst communities grow around them.

The Tree That Owns Itself
In 1890, American newspaper *Athens Weekly Banner* detailed how a landowner deeded an old tree and the surrounding land to itself. While there is no evidence of this deed, locals have treated it with reverence, even replacing the tree after it died in the 1940s. Today 'The Son of The Tree That Owns Itself' stands in the same Georgian plot adorned with a tasteful wall, chain and a very worn plaque.

Wish Tree
When a tree reaches an ancient age or is distinguished by strange features, visitors may begin treating it as a 'wish tree'. This tradition is observed spontaneously all over the world. In Antipaxos, Greece tourists leave their names or wishes written on stones around an ancient pine. In Scotland, Ireland and Wales there are *Clootie* trees, which visitors adorn with beads and ribbons.

WORSE HAS HAPPENED AT SEA

The vast and temperamental oceans are an optimal stew for urban legends. There is a tale for every sunken ship, roaring leviathan and unusual watery fate.

Unlucky Mummy

In the late 19th century, journalist William Stead spread a rumour in British newspapers that Englishman Douglas Murray bought himself a cursed mummy that caused storms, deaths and illness. Stead soon died during the sinking of the RMS *Titanic*, leading some to blame the mummy. In reality the artefact the tale is based on is an ornate coffin lid, and was never owned by Murray.

Who Goes There?

Since the 1930s there has been a tale of a ship that lost its way in the fog. The skipper peered over the railings and was shocked to see another man yards away, standing behind his own set of railings.

'You fool, watch where you're going with that ship!' cried the skipper. 'This isn't a bloody ship, this is a lighthouse!' replied the lighthouse keeper.

The tale first appears in Canadian newspaper *The Drumheller Review* in 1931. Intended as a joke, the story has frequently circulated as a true story. The confused ship has been depicted as everything from a steamship to a US Navy aircraft carrier.

HOLLOW EARTH

Many mythologies and religions reference an underworld (such as Hades in Greek myth), however in the world of urban legends, even the very ground beneath our feet can be a source of suspicion and rumour.

As Above, So Below
In the 1930s, American engineer George Warren Shufelt went in search of an underground city of lizard people below Los Angeles using an X-ray machine. As far as we know, Shufelt never found his lizards, but the theory has caught on in the conspiracy world.

Byrd is the Word
Richard E. Byrd was an American aviator and explorer who made five Polar expeditions between 1928 and 1956. In the 1950s, conspiracy theorists alleged Byrd had found the entrance to a secret land under the Antarctic. The theory was popularised by American ufologist Walter Siegmeister in his book *The Hollow Earth* (1964). While the hollow earth conspiracy was initially limited to UFO and occult literature, it has since been spread by the internet and films like *Godzilla: King of Monsters* (2019).

A diagram of the Earth, according to hollow Earth enthusiasts.

 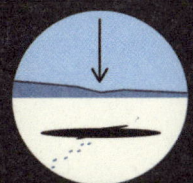    

In fiction, the inner Earth provides a backdrop to daring adventures.

WARTIME LEGENDS

The terror and paranoia of war is a catalyst for many rumours and legends. Some rumours are encouraged to bolster morale, while others are used to direct hatred towards the enemy.

Foo Fighters
During the Second World War, pilots saw lights around their aircraft. Many assumed they were new aerial weapons and nicknamed them 'Foo Fighters'. After the war, the phenomena was folded into the new interest in UFOs. Most skeptics believe the lights were caused by the rare weather phenomena called St. Elmo's fire.

Gremlins

British Royal Airforce crews blamed 'gremlins' for mechanical failures in the Second World War. Light-hearted newspaper articles and safety posters depicted them as small elf-like people, and some crews painted gremlins onto their planes for good luck.

According to ufologist Robert Coe Gardner, a US Air Force plane was forced to land in 1939 following a gremlin attack. Allegedly, the ground crew entered the plane to find twelve dead crewmen and a strong smell of sulphur. Despite the lack of evidence, this story is often circulated as true.

Pérák The Springman

During the Nazi occupation of Czechoslovakia, the local resistance was believed to have a costumed superhero among their ranks. Pérák was restyled as a heroic thorn in the side of Nazi occupiers. The short animated film *Pérák a SS* (1946) brought the figure to a wider audience. The Springman has since been used as a patriotic symbol across the political spectrum.

MYSTERIOUS DISAPPEARANCES

Around the world, mysterious disappearances have captivated people's attention. After all, where uncertainty lies, speculation flourishes.

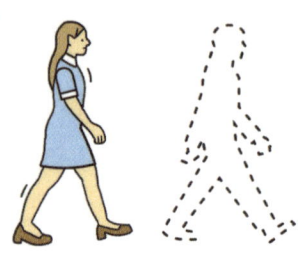

Louis Le Prince
French inventor Louis Le Prince is credited for making the first film camera in 1888. In 1890, he mysteriously disappeared on his way to Paris. Some believe he was assassinated by agents of American inventor, Thomas Edison, to steal his invention (Edison's lab finished making their camera a few years later).

Le Prince's Camera

Amelia Earhart
American aviator Amelia Earhart was the first woman to fly solo across the Atlantic Ocean. On 2 July, 1937, she disappeared with her navigator Fred Noonan during an attempted flight around the world. The official theory is that the plane ran out of fuel and crashed. Other theories include alien abduction.

Harold Holt
Holt served as Prime Minister of Australia from 1966 until his disappearance in 1967 when he vanished under the waves on Cheviot Beach. Despite a thorough search, his body was never recovered. Some believe Holt was spirited away by foreign spies, criminals or a submarine. Most people accept Holt died in an unfortunate drowning.

D. B. Cooper

On 24 November 1971, a man travelling under the name Dan Cooper (later known as D. B. Cooper) hijacked a plane flying to Seattle, USA. With the threat of an apparent bomb, Cooper exchanged passengers for $200,000 and four parachutes at Seattle airport. With no one harmed and cash in hand, Cooper instructed the crew to take him back to the skies where he parachuted from the plane, never to be seen again. Cooper's mystery identity has spawned a number of urban legends, leading amateur sleuths to stalk alleged suspects.

D. B. Cooper   The Alleged Bomb

MIDCENTURY

Volume 336 of Argosy magazine, 1968.

CRYPTOZOOLOGY

The study of legendary animals, or cryptids, is known as cryptozoology. Pioneering cryptozoologists in the early 20th century were encouraged by famous discoveries of animals people once believed to be legend. Examples included the okapi, formally documented in 1901, and the Komodo dragon, officially named and described in 1912. In the absence of conventional evidence, cryptozoology usually relies on witnesses, photographs and footprints. For this reason, it is not widely considered a formal science.

Monkey Business

Around 1920, Swiss oil geologist François de Loys and company surveyed the Tarra river on the fringes of Venezuela. There, they were apparently attacked by large monkeys unknown to science. A photo of one of the animals was widely circulated and drew a lot of speculation. It has long been decided the photo was hoaxed to support fringe theories about evolution.

Legend, Myth?

Cryptids can range from the unlikely survivors of extinction to fantastical monsters and creatures from religion and myth. Often, the only thing that unites them under the homogeneity of cryptozoology are the editorial decisions of enthusiasts.

Nandi Bear

The Nandi people in Kenya once told stories of a legendary bear known by a number of names, such as Duba (from the Arabic word for bear). Locals described it as 4 foot high, reddish-brown and very ferocious. Sightings of the animal diminished in the 20th century and no certain evidence of its existence has ever been found.

On the Track of Unknown Animals

From the 1950s, French-Belgian explorer Bernard Heuvelmans popularised cryptozoology. He was quite a character, having earned a zoological doctorate studying aardvark teeth, escaped a Nazi prison camp and befriended Tintin creator Hergé. His book *On the Track of Unknown Animals* (1958) exhaustively listed legendary creatures like the Australian Bunyip and the Himalayan Yeti.

Bigfoot, North America

Mammoth, Russia

Giant Anaconda, South America

Bunyip, Australia

Cryptozoologists Today

Like ufologists and ghost hunters, cryptozoologists seem to be predominately white, male and American. The demographics are perhaps a result of Western popular culture influences – particularly science fiction and game hunting. Looking for cryptids can also be costly as it requires specialised equipment. Income is mostly generated through books, sales, TV and streaming appearances, and the sale of merchandise.

YETI

The untamed wilderness, and the hairy things that may dwell within, have always inspired fear and rumour. The legendary ape-creature *Yeti*, derived from a Tibetan word meaning 'animal of rocky places', is just one of many similar stories. In Mongolia, there are tales of hairy men called Almas and in China there are the Yeren, tall creatures who laugh with delight when encountering humans.

Abominable Snowman
In 1921, a British expedition found the tracks of a large animal high in the Himalayan mountains. A local Sherpa on the team explained the footprints belonged to a *metoh-kangmi* (meaning wild man of the snow). Upon their return, *The Statesman* journalist Henry Newman applied artistic license and dubbed it the Abominable Snowman.

Brown, White and Red?
Sightings of Yeti usually purport it to be brown-furred. The popular image of the white Yeti was largely spread by artistic license.

Fresh Prints
In 1951, English mountaineer Eric Shipton took photographs of apparent Yeti footprints during his attempted scaling of Everest. Skeptics have suggested they were either a hoax or animal tracks distorted by melting snow. Newspaper reports featuring these photographs created a new interest in the Yeti.

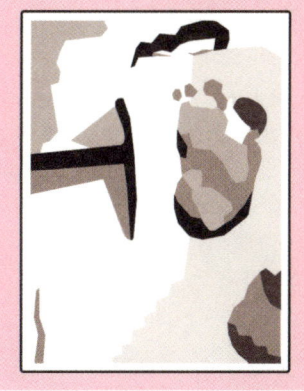

Open Season
In 1954, British newspaper *The Daily Mail* funded an expedition to find the Yeti. Among other activities, the team examined a reputed Yeti scalp kept in a Buddhist temple. Anatomist Frederick Wood Jones later identified the scalp as the shoulder of a yak or goat.

CIA Man
American businessman Tom Slick used his wealth to fund searches for cryptids. His Himalayan expeditions were able to prove that some Yeti skins were in fact bear pelts. As Slick had curious links to the CIA, some believe his expeditions were used as a clever excuse to spy on China.

Bear With Me
Skeptics generally believe Yeti-like legends in the region were originally inspired by brown bears and rogue bandits. Regardless, the Yeti has firmly earned a place in popular culture, appearing in everything from Disneyland rides to the Pixar film *Monsters Inc.* (2001).

ROAD RUMOURS

Whether it is suspicious hitchhikers or menacing cars, roads are home to a great many urban legends.

The Hook
As it goes, one night a young couple were relaxing in their car when they heard a report on the radio. An escaped criminal was on the loose, distinguished only by a prosthetic hook. Frightened, the lovers drove home. Upon exiting their car, they were shocked to discover a hook jammed in the car door. The escapee had tried to break in!

This story has been in circulation since the 1950s. It is typical of urban legends that express a prejudice or discomfort with bodily injuries and disabilities. It was likely inspired by murders in 'Lovers Lane' areas such as the Texarkana Moonlight Murders in 1946.

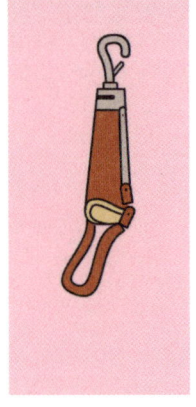

A Helping Hand
Prosthetic hooks are still used by many people today. Some are perfect for exercising and can help pick up heavy weights.

Black Volga
According to legend, the streets of 1960s Eastern Europe were once stalked by evil black Volga cars. The cars would cruise up to lone pedestrians and assailants would jump out and kidnap them. The kidnapper's identity varies with each telling, ranging from thieves to the Devil himself. Sadly, there may be some truth to the abductions. Polish journalist Przemysław Semczuk documented a number of cases in which people were snatched from the street by unknown drivers.

The Phantom Hitchhiker
This popular story, told all over the world, begins with a driver kindly giving a hitchhiker a lift home. When he arrived at their destination, the driver was astounded to discover their passenger had vanished. Fearing an accident, the driver knocked on the hitchhiker's home door and was met by an elderly resident. The resident explained that a person matching the hitchhiker's description had died some years ago. In 1942, American folklorists Richard Beardsley and Rosalie Hankey published a study comparing 79 versions of the story told around the USA. It was found, despite variations in detail and setting, they mostly conformed to the same sort of story and twist.

UFOs

The term 'Unidentified Flying Object' was invented by the US Air Force during their investigations of the flying saucer phenomena in the 1950s. UFO reports can encompass everything from distant lights to close encounters with alien interlopers.

Generally speaking, urban legends feature abstract characters, while UFOs are (usually) seen by real people. Speculation and reportage, however, can distort UFO sightings until they become dismissed as urban legend.

UFO Shapes

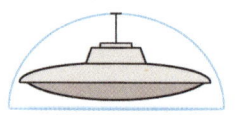
Sweden (1946)

Brazil (1947)

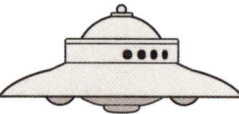
USA (1952)

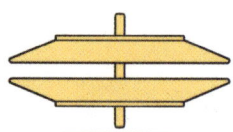
Italy (1952)

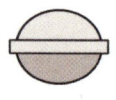
Brazil (1976)

France (1989)

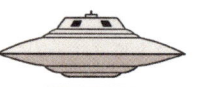
USA (1989)

USA (2004)

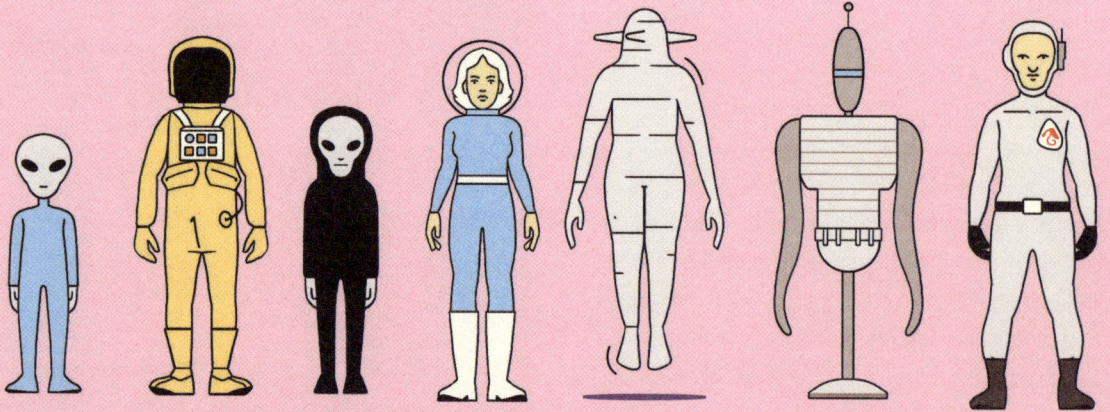

Witnesses have reported a wide variety of UFO inhabitants, or *ufonauts*, ranging from the familiar to the alien.

The Roswell Incident

Easily the most famous UFO case occurred in 1947 when an American rancher reported the discovery of strange debris in the desert in New Mexico, USA. The local air force base in Roswell recovered the materials and prematurely released a statement on their capture of a 'flying disc'. Soon, however, they released another statement to clarify that the debris in fact belonged to a crashed weather balloon.

In the years following, supposed witnesses, hoaxers and ufologists have contributed to the legend, adding details about dead aliens, military cover-ups and secret experiments. Today, Roswell is teeming with UFO tourist attractions, including museums and a flying saucer-shaped McDonald's.

Secret Bases

The UFO phenomena also inspires localised urban legends of government coverups, facilities and crash sites. The air force testing site *Area 51* in Nevada, USA became associated with UFOs as far back as the 1950s. Over the years, increasingly colourful legends of the base harboring live aliens and reverse-engineered flying saucers have attracted a regular pilgrimage of legend trippers. More niche alleged UFO facilities include the archives in Vatican City, and RAF Woodbridge in the UK.

ODD ATTRACTIONS

Monuments to engineered fun, parks and attractions are host to all manner of urban legends lurking among their brightly painted rides and buildings.

Ghosts of Disneyland

In Disneyland, USA it is said the ghost of a construction worker haunts the Pirates of the Caribbean ride. Allegedly, there is a tradition among park staff to wish the ghost a goodnight upon closing the ride each day. The legend was re-popularised in 2022, when a TikTok medium recounted a supposed encounter with the ghost.

Doomed Boat Lovers

In Inokashira Park, Tokyo, visitors may rent boats to row around the lake. According to legend, couples who ride together are doomed to break up. It is thought the nearby shrine to goddess Benzaiten is envious of their love and can bring about their emotional downfall.

Welcome to Crocodile Park
On the island of Bali, Indonesia stands a theme park that has been abandoned since the year 2000. Tourists visit Taman Festival Park to enjoy the spectacle of a huge amusement park being slowly swallowed up by the forest. Locals have circulated an urban legend that says, upon closure, the park owners left the resident crocodiles to roam free. They have since been seen by unwitting sightseers.

The park has become an ever-changing backdrop for graffiti artists, tourists, photographers and influencers.

MEDIA LEGENDS

Celebrities are a common target for salacious rumours, ranging from faked deaths to peculiar eccentricities.

Walt Disney's Frozen

Shortly after the death of American animation legend Walt Disney in 1966, rumours surfaced that his corpse had been frozen until he could be resurrected by future technology. The first printed reference to this appeared in a 1969 edition of the French magazine *Ici Paris*, in which the rumours were dismissed as being spread by disgruntled employees. There is a modern bolt-on conspiracy theory that the Disney film *Frozen* (2013) was produced to redirect internet traffic from the search terms 'Disney' and 'frozen'.

London Cawing

Persistent urban legends blame the invasive flocks of parakeets in London, UK, on the extravagances of celebrities, including Jimi Hendrix and George Michael. Some even believe they escaped from the film set of *The African Queen* (1951). In reality, the birds have been in the UK since the 19th century. It is likely the flocks are the result of escapes from private aviaries over the years.

Paul McCartney Doppelgänger

Allegedly, Beatles member Paul McCartney died in a car crash in 1966 and was secretly replaced. Fringe theorists believe MI5 recruited a look-alike to avoid public mourning. Proponents claimed the Beatles hid clues about McCartney's supposed demise in their creative output. Fans, radio DJs and reporters encouraged the speculation and often bothered Beatles members (particularly McCartney) about the ridiculous rumours.

Curious Clues

The Beatles' album *Abbey Road* (1969) was supposed by theorists to show the band posing as funeral mourners – George as a grave digger, Paul the deceased, Ringo the undertaker and John as Jesus or a clergyman. McCartney parodied the theory with the cover of his solo album *Paul is Live* (1993), featuring himself in the same location with a dog.

  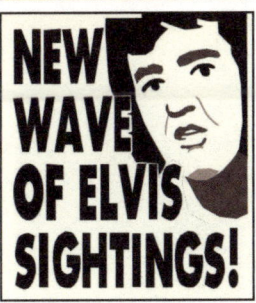 

Elvis is Alive

Following his death in 1977, some believed Elvis Presley had faked his own death following sightings of him in unlikely locations. The earliest report said that Elvis was seen at Memphis Airport buying a ticket to Buenos Aires. In reality, the airport did not offer tickets to Buenos Aires at the time. Over the years, dodgy photos and witness testimonies about Elvis have been circulated in satirical newspapers like the *Weekly World News*.

PHENOMENA

Strange phenomena, from mysterious sounds to spontaneous combustion, have caused speculation for centuries. Though skeptics offer simple explanations, some people have created more unlikely paranormal reasons for their occurrence.

Weird Artefacts
There are many historic objects with legendary attributes. The 1996 Svetlana Telets painting 'The Rain Woman' is said to be cursed.

Teleportation
In one 16th century case, a soldier from the Philippines was recorded to have suddenly appeared in Mexico.

Spontaneous Human Combustion
A supposed event in which people suddenly burst into flames. In reality, most are tragic cases of people with limited mobility catching fire after dropping a cigarette.

Cattle Mutilation
Since the 70s, American farmers have reported livestock being killed and drained of blood. Aliens have been blamed, but it's likely the fault of birds, coyotes and insects.

Objects from the Sky

Throughout history, there have been sightings of random objects falling from the sky, including frogs, fish and small animals. In 2018, residents of the Fazilpur Badli village in India were startled when a 10kg chunk of ice thudded to Earth. It was strongly suspected to be frozen urine dumped from a passing aeroplane.

Stones That Move (Slowly)

In Death Valley, USA, there are rocks that seem to move on their own. After a century of research, it was found that the rocks are actually pushed by winds across a thin layer of ice.

The Hum

Since the 1970s, there have been reports of phantom humming, similar to that of a large machine. Skeptics have blamed mass-hysteria, animals and industrial machinery.

FREAKY FATALITIES

Urban legends could be one way human beings explore their fears and anxieties about death. These tales enforce social anxieties about everyday hazards, both realistic and fantastical.

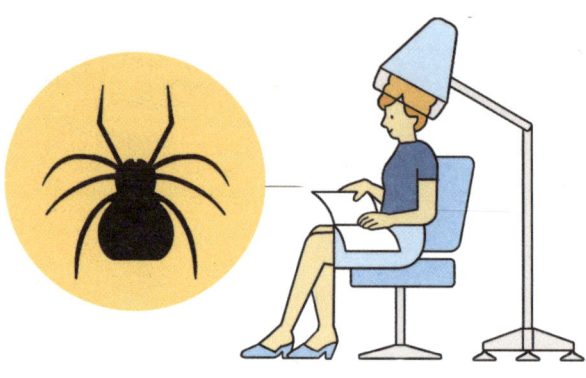

Horrid Hairdo
A teen treated herself to a bouffant hairdo at a salon. At school, she felt a dull pain followed by nausea and promptly collapsed dead at her desk. Doctors were shocked to find an infestation of black widow spiders in her hair. This legend may have originated in 1950s America, but has different tellings around the world, each concerning a different hairdo.

Fan Death
In South Korea, some believe that leaving an electric cooling fan on overnight can cause death through chill or lack of oxygen. This legend originated in the 1920s, when the fans were first introduced, and likely spawned from a fear of new technology. As a result, electric fans sold in South Korea often include an automatic timer.

Off With Their Head
In some countries there is a legend of a motorcyclist who was speeding along the motorway when a sheet of glass slipped off a truck and decapitated them. Another version of the tale from the 1960s concerns the Phantom Motorcyclist of Elmore, an American ghost motorcyclist who is said to lurk around a bridge where they were beheaded.

Up the Wrong Tree

In the 1980s, a story circulated that French firefighters trawling through the aftermath of a forest fire were astounded to find a dead scuba diver in a tree. Supposedly, the diver had been accidentally dropped there by a fire-fighting helicopter (which sucked him up when filling up its tank in a lake). However, no known incident has appeared in record, and water bombers lack pipes large enough to slurp up a whole person.

BIGFOOT

Bigfoot originated in Native American cultures and, like Yeti, it is an amalgamation of many folklore characters. Native American tales of wild and hairy men share commonalities with other stories from around the world, such as the Yowie in Australia or Orange Mawas in Malaysia.

Yowie, Australia

Orange Mawas, Malaysia

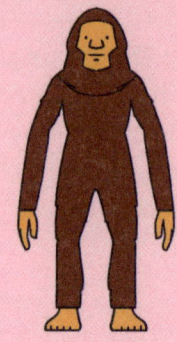
Nguoi Rung, Vietnam

Sasquatch
Sasquatch is the anglicised Sts'ailes name for a bigfoot-like entity (*sasq'ets*). Since 1938 the Sts'ailes people in Canada and the Northern USA have held a 'Sasquatch Day' to celebrate their community. Today, the festival features canoe races, costumes and food.

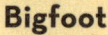

Ape Canyon Incident
In 1924, the periodical *The Oregonian* shared the news of an alleged battle between gold prospectors and 'ape-men' near Mount St. Helens. To this day the area is known as Ape Canyon. There is no physical evidence that the event took place.

Bigfoot
In 1958, construction workers Raymond Wallace and Jerry Crew showed plaster casts of big footprints to the press. Newspapers excitedly ran with the mystery of 'Bigfoot', coining the name. Skeptics believe the footprints were faked with large wooden stamps.

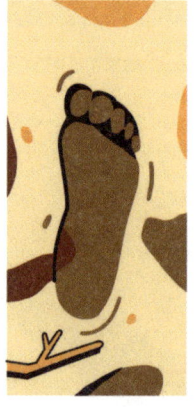

Walk on the Wild Side

In 1967, filmmaker and cowboy duo Roger Patterson and Bob Gilmin provided evidence in the form of a 59-second film showing an ape-like creature walking through a clearing (informally known as the Patty film). Skeptics believe the footage shows a man in a home-built suit, while proponents still uphold it as the best evidence of Bigfoot.

Bigfoot enthusiasts (occasionally known to some as bigfooters) are still very much engaged in the search for the elusive animal to this day.

Besides footprint casts and photos, hunters collect possible hair samples that often belong to known animals like wolves, bears and racoons.

Like ufologists and ghost hunters, bigfooters range in skepticism and devout belief. They are also split by the ethics of killing a bigfoot, if only to prove it is real.

SPACE STORIES

Space explorations are subject to a number of rumours and conspiracies, usually based on ignorance and suspicion.

Phantom Cosmonauts
In the early years of the 20th century space race, Western newspapers alleged that the Soviet Union had covered up the deaths of several cosmonauts in space. In the 1960s, Italian amateur radio operators publicised their alleged recordings of dying cosmonauts. While skeptics believe the recordings to be fake, they are a subject of fringe conspiracies.

Channels, Faces and Pyramids of Mars
Over the years, a number of curiosities photographed on the Martian surface bolstered a fringe theory that the planet had once supported an alien civilisation. Modern high-quality photographs have since showed that the features were the result of optical illusions caused by ambiguous shapes in photos taken with low-resolution equipment.

Skeleton on the Moon
Supposedly, a Chinese astrophysicist once announced their discovery of a jean-wearing skeleton on the Moon. This ridiculous yarn was invented by the *Weekly World News*, a tabloid that published mostly fictional 'news' stories in the USA between 1979 and 2007. Their stories often covered supernatural themes and their approach was usually satirical.

Space Pen

In legend, NASA spent millions of dollars inventing a pen that could be used by astronauts in zero gravity. After months of development they presented the space-pen to their counterparts in the Soviet space program. Unimpressed, the Soviets replied, 'We use pencils'. In reality, early manned missions used mechanical pencils, which were deemed risky and expensive. In 1965 the Fisher Pen Company designed a space pen (costing under $3 each) used by both NASA and Soviets.

Moon Mania

In 1969, NASA successfully landed astronauts on the Moon. Fringe theorists soon cast doubt on the extraordinary accomplishment, despite live television broadcasts, subsequent scientific advances, five additional successful missions and the thousands of staff involved. Theorists believed the Moon landings were faked in a film studio for propaganda purposes. Their scrutiny is mainly based on searching NASA's photographs and films for signs of fakery. Folklorists have suggested the cynical theory was encouraged by a distrust of the US government during the Vietnam War, and following the infamous Watergate scandal.

MOTHMAN

Since ancient times there have been tales of flying humanoids. In Thai folklore, the Krahang is a ghostly man who is said to fly by flapping rice baskets. In 1884, Reynard Beck from Missouri, USA, supposedly woke up one morning with the ability to float around. One of the more famous legends of flying humanoids is the Point Pleasant Mothman.

Owlman, UK

Ahool, Indonesia

Jetpack Man, USA

Flight of Fancy

On the 1st November, 1966, a national guardsman in Point Pleasant, WV, USA was startled by what he described as a man in a brown outfit perched on a high tree branch. On the 15th, two young couples were driving along and caught a glimpse of a man with red eyes and large wings. As they drove away in panic, the creature pursued them at speeds of up to 100mph. This latter encounter made its way into the local newspaper *Point Pleasant Register* under the headline 'Couples See Man-Sized Bird... Creature... Something!'.

More sightings followed, usually in the Point Pleasant area. Witnesses described a winged man or large bird lurking on roofs and chasing cars. The moniker 'Mothman' eventually became favoured in reportage and rumour mills.

The Bridge

On the 15th December 1967, a large suspension bridge in Point Pleasant collapsed, tragically killing 46 people. While locals mourned one of the worst bridge disasters in US history, some spread rumours that the Mothman had been their omen of doom. Ufologists John Keel and Gray Barker interviewed witnesses and introduced their own questionable details about the event. Keel's book, *The Mothman Prophecies* (1975), spread the legend internationally.

TNT Area

Some of the more colourful Mothman sightings were centralised near an old ammunition facility, which locals call the TNT Area. The power plant building, the most distinctive ruin in the area, succumbed to demolition in the 1990s following years of trespassing by locals and tourists.

A Star is Born

While the original sightings suggested the creature was bird-like, depictions of Mothman across media lean well into the moth moniker. Artists tend to show Mothman with antennae and insectoid wings.

Mothman merchandise

Annual Mothman Festival attendees

Mothman Statue, Point Pleasant

POSTMODERN ERA

A film adaption of common home invasion legends, Black Christmas, 1974.

HOME INVADERS

If the home is a place of comfort and safety, it is unsurprising that the fear of being watched and besieged in one's home is the basis of several urban legends.

The Caller
The story goes, a babysitter received a telephone call from a scary voice. The frightened babysitter called the police, who promised to trace the call. After another creepy message, the police quickly returned her call and instructed her to leave the house immediately. Outside, she was met by a squad of police officers, who informed her that the call had come from inside the house.

Some believe the story originated in 1960s America, and was inspired by real burglaries and murders. The tale has inspired horror films such as *Black Christmas* (1976) and *Scream* (1996).

The Licked Hand

In the legend, a young woman had trouble sleeping one night and reached her hand into the darkness to pat her pet dog. Comforted by the feeling of licking, she soon fell asleep. When morning came she was horrified to discover a message on the wall reading 'Humans can lick too'. The tale is remarkably similar to the short story The Diary of Mr. Poynter (1919) by English author M. R. James.

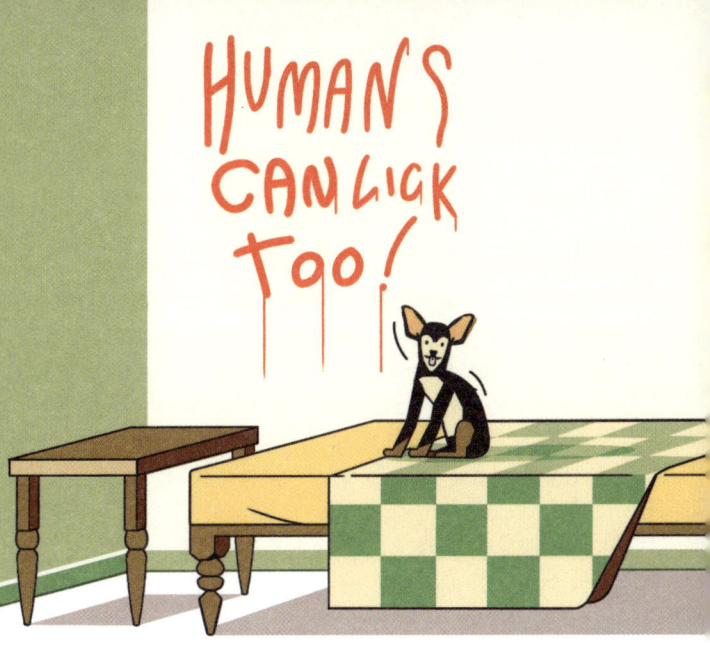

Gap Woman

In legend, Sukima-onna (Japanese for gap woman) is a paranormal entity that lurks in the darkest recesses of your home. She is said to peer from between curtains, under the bed and even from the slightest gap between wall and cupboard. The story was circulated in Japan during the early 2000s but may be much older.

Slippery Bandits

During the 1990s in Karachi, Pakistan, there was a rumoured gang of burglars called the Chadda Group. The thieves supposedly operated in their underwear and covered themselves in oil to evade detection and capture.

CREEPY CONTAMINATION

Some tales explore the common fear of dangerous, even fatal, ingredients making their way into the human body. Swedish scientist, Jan Bondeson, found 68 medical records dating back to the 17th century about patients who believed they had live reptiles and amphibians living inside them.

Poisoned Dress
In one 1940s telling, an American woman became ill after wearing a second-hand dress. It was soon discovered the dress was laced with poisonous formaldehyde, having formally being worn by a corpse. This story has echoes of ancient tales about poisoned clothes, like the *Shirt of Fire* in Greek myth, which in some versions was used to murder the hero Hercules.

Mouse in Coke
According to legend, a person won a large payout by the Coca-Cola company after finding a dead mouse in a freshly bought bottle. This legend has been in circulation for decades and was likely inspired by real attempted lawsuits against soft drink companies. In the USA, between 1910 and 1994, there were at least 47 reported litigations about rodents appearing in soft drinks.

Gruesome Gum
The launch of the American Bubble Yum chewing gum in 1976 faced difficulty following rumours that the gum contained spider eggs. The rumours probably started because people were suspicious of how soft the gum was. Rumours were so widespread that Bubble Yum's parent company paid for advertisements to restore consumer faith.

Yucky Yucca
In another arachnophobic yarn, it was claimed that cactus plants bought at British department store Marks & Spencer concealed dozens of tarantula eggs. Supposedly the eggs lay dormant until one day the cactus exploded into a cloud of huge angry spiders. In reality, tarantulas take years to grow and are not known to leave their eggs in flora. The tale was circulated in the 1980s, but is similar to other spider legends.

Fast Food Faux Pas
Some of the better known contamination legends focus their accusations on fast food franchises. From the 1970s, it was rumoured that a KFC restaurant in the USA had unwittingly served a fried rat. In 2015, the rumour resurfaced on Facebook, accompanied by a hoaxed image of a suspiciously-rat shaped chicken fillet.

GALLERY OF CRYPTIDS

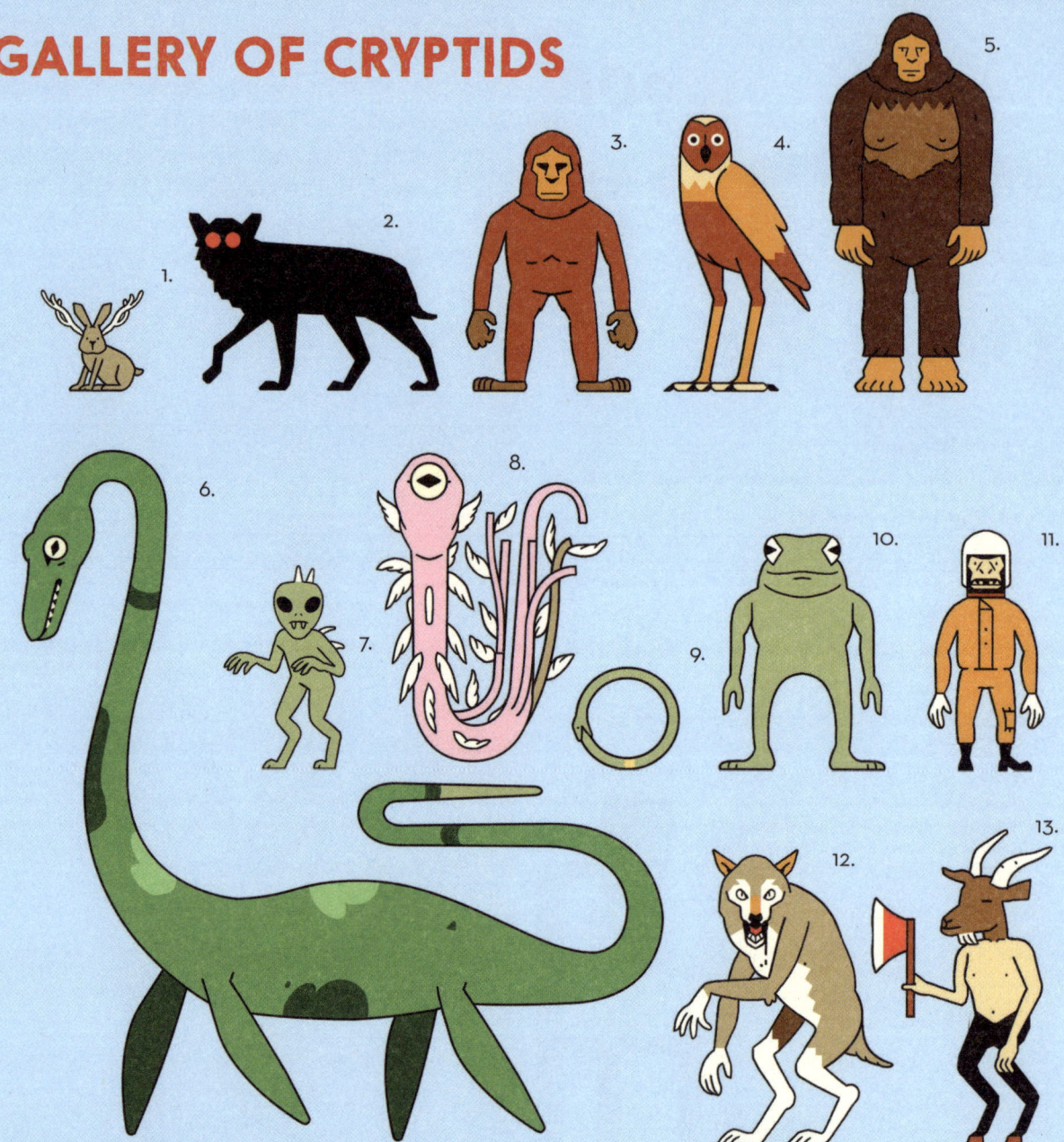

Cryptids are legendary animals that cryptozoologists believe may exist in the world, but are not recognised by science. As there's no formal governance to decide what qualifies as a cryptid, some researchers have chosen to include mythical animals, aliens and even ghosts.

1. Jackalope, North America
2. Black Shuck, UK
3. Almas, Russia
4. Chickcharney, Andros Island
5. Bigfoot, North America
6. Loch Ness Monster, UK
7. Chupacabra, Mexico
8. Crawfordsville Monster, USA
9. Hoopsnake, USA

10. Loveland Frogman, USA
11. Monkey Man, India
12. Dogman, USA
13. Pope Lick Monster, USA
14. Mongolian Death Worm, Gobi Desert
15. Nandi bear, Kenya
16. Yeti, Himalayas
17. Orang Pendek, Indonesia
18. Human (for scale)
19. Kongamato, Zambia, Congo
20. Barmanou, Pakistan
21. Hibagon, Japan
22. Squonk, USA
23. Mothman, USA
24. Lizardman, USA
25. Orang Bati, Indonesia
26. Alien Big Cat, UK
27. Yowie, Australia

YOU HAD TO BE THERE

While many urban legends skew towards horror, some more closely resemble jokes. The humour can be derived from a slapstick scenario or even the absurdity of the tale itself.

Barrel of Bricks
Circa 1960s, Vietnam. Akin to cartoon physics, a builder was allegedly flung into the air by a barrel of bricks. The oldest version can be found in an American newspaper from 1895, but it is likely much older.

Dragged Roofer
Circa 1960s, South Africa. A roofer ties his safety rope to the bumper of his wife's car and is dragged down the street. This story may have originated in the satirical newspaper *Weekly World News*.

Rattle in the Cadillac
Circa 1960s, USA. A car owner allegedly discovered the annoying rattle in their car was an act of sabotage from a disgruntled factory worker. Popularised by an anecdote shared by American footballer Brian Bosworth in 1986. General Motors denied it had ever happened.

 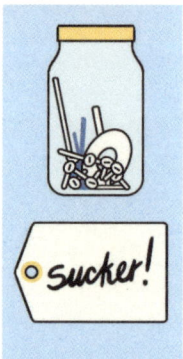

Kangaroo Calamity
Circa 1980s, Australia. In legend, tourists driving in the outback encountered a large kangaroo and posed with it for pictures. The driver dropped the animal in their jacket, and it immediately hopped off, with the car keys still in the pocket. The tale is likely made up.

Barometer Question
Circa 1990s, Japan. During a lesson, a student worked out the height of the building by throwing a barometer out of the window. There are numerous versions told around the world, but it likely originates from the American magazine *Reader's Digest* in 1958.

Exploding Toilet
Circa 1990s, Germany. Allegedly a man threw a lit cigarette in the toilet, unaware that it had been filled with a highly flammable substance. Decades later, in 2004, a man in West Virginia, USA filed a lawsuit alleging that a leaky gas pipe caused his portable toilet to explode.

Runaway Grandma
Circa 1940s, USA. An urban legend in which an old woman died during a long road trip. The grieving family stowed her body on the car's roof rack and wrapped her in whatever came to hand. After stopping for a break, the family returned to find the car (and the granny) vanished.

THE STRANGER

Some urban legends are focused on strangers and the threats they seem to pose to us. These stories expose how fear is so often inspired by the unknown and social anxieties.

Bunnyman

Since the 1970s, a legend has told that the Colchester Overpass in Clifton, USA was once guarded by a man in a rabbit costume. Local archivist Brian A. Conley discovered two 1970 police reports alleging that a man in such a costume had threatened people with a hatchet.

Known as Bunnyman Bridge, it was believed that the Bunnyman would attack teenagers around Halloween. The site is a common attraction for teenagers, in what academics call legend tripping, and in 2011, law enforcements turned away a group of 200 visitors to the site.

Men in Black

Since the 1940s, people have reported encounters with eerie people wearing dark clothes. These strangers are known for stalking UFO witnesses and dissuading them from sharing their stories. Some believe the tales are based on real cases of UFO witnesses being visited by FBI agents and ufologists.

Visitor to W. D. Clendenon, 1961

Visitor to Mary Hyre, 1967

Visitor to David Ellis, 1981

Aka Manto

In legend, Aka Manto (Japanese for Red Cloak), is a ghost, man or monster said to haunt bathrooms. Aka Manto offers toilet cubicle users a choice between red and blue toilet paper. Supposedly, the only way to escape a horrible death is to refuse or run away. Some folklorists believe the tale has origins in rumours of a cloaked man in Osaka City during the 1930s.

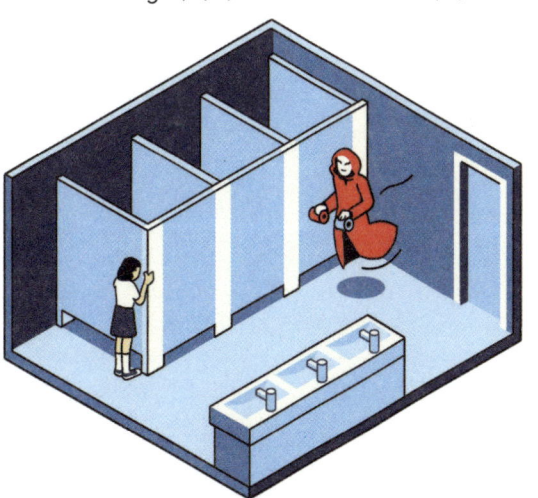

Hollow-Eyed Woman
A haunter of Korean roads, who in legend approaches drivers to reveal empty eye sockets hidden under sunglasses.

Teketeke
A Japanese legend, dating to the 1940s. It is told the ghost was cut in half by a train, and attacks people with a bladed weapon.

Serbian Dancing Lady
A legend possibly made up by TikTok users. Since the 2010s an eerie dancing lady is believed to attack onlookers.

XEROXLORE

Before the internet, many people used photocopiers to spread urban legends. Legend-carrying posters appeared on office cork boards, walls and lampposts. People made copies of copies, causing their image quality to degrade over time.

So, here it is, and please pass it to someone else or run a few copies... I paid for it; now you can have it for free...

- 2 cups butter
- 2 tsp baking soda
- 5 cups oatmeal
- 2 cups brown sugar
- 1 8oz Hershey bar
- 2 tsp baking powder
- 2 tsp vanilla
- 4 cups flour
- 2 cups sugar
- 24 oz chocolate chips
- 1 tsp salt
- 4 eggs
- 2 cups chopped nuts

Cream butter and sugars. Add eggs and vanilla, mix with flour, oatmeal, salt, baking powder, and baking soda. Add chocolate & nuts. Roll into ball and bake for 10 minutes at 375 degrees. Makes 112 cookies.

Cookie recipe, $250 – Variations of this fable have been going around for nearly a century. The recipe now appears on numerous recipe and food blogs.

SATANIC PROCTOR AND GAMBLE!

Watch out for the SATANIC SYMBOL found on the front or back of all their products. Christians should always remember that if they buy any products with this symbol they are taking part in the support of the Church of Satan or devil worship!

Satanic panic – Poster spreading a false rumour about Procter & Gamble (circa 1980s).

Get well soon!

A nine-year-old cancer patient wanted to break the record for having received the most greetings cards. Poster and email appeals for cards became distorted through urban legend, leading to many cards arriving at wrong or fictional addresses. (circa 1990s).

HELP JIMMY BREAK THE WORLD RECORD!

Jimmy is nine years old and bravely fighting cancer. We want to break the world record for most GET WELL SOON cards, please send as many as you can to the following address:

3 Acacia Avenue
Chipping Cleghorn
England

ATTENTION!!! ATTENTION!!!

PLEASE BE ADVISED, "ACME POP" & "ATOMIC PUNCH" ARE BEING MANUFACTURED BY THE KLU.. KLUX.. KLAN..

PLEASE COPY AND PASS IT ON!

YOU HAVE BEEN WARNED
SAVE THE CHILDREN!

Please be aware of the following: Police Departments across the nation are being warned of this gang initiation. Their intent is to have all new gang members nationwide drive around on Saturday and Sunday night with their headlights off. In order to be accepted into the gang, they have to shoot and kill all individuals in the first car that does a courtesy flash to warn them that their lights are off.

Chain letter – Hoax letters and emails that encourage the recipient to further spread the message (circa 1990s).

Lights off – A poster warning road users about gang activity (circa 1990s).

ANIMAL ANTICS

In urban legends, pets and animals are frequent targets of dark humour, accidents and imagined dangers.

Hot Dog
In this legend, an old woman tried using her brand-new microwave to dry off her rain-soaked pet. Tragically, she killed the dog in the process. This tale surfaced in 1970s America when microwaves became affordable to the mass market. It is a simple tale that conjures fears of new technology and the frailties of old age.

The Choking Doberman
The tale goes that a woman came home to find her dog choking. At the vets, she was told the dog would need surgery and she ought to wait at home. Soon after, the vet called on the telephone and frantically warned her to leave the house. It turned out the dog was choking on severed fingers, having attacked a burglar who was hiding in the woman's cupboard. This version of the tale circulated in America in the 1980s, but has probably been around much longer.

Bump in the Rug
Taking a moment to admire their work, a contractor noticed a small bump in the carpet. Assuming they had left a cigarette box under the carpet, they took a hammer and bashed the bump until it was flat. Later, the homeowner returned and asked if they had seen their pet hamster. In a moment of horrid realisation, the contractor noticed the missing cigarettes on the kitchen counter. This tale may have originated in a 1964 edition of *Reader's Digest* magazine.

Later Alligator
It has often been said that New York sewers are infested with Florida alligators. Supposedly, baby reptiles were brought back by holidaymakers and were flushed down the toilet when they got tiresome. In reality, alligators are unlikely to survive long in sewage. The story has been shared in New York periodicals since the 1930s, but it is similar to 19th century tales of feral hogs living in London sewers.

GOING UNDERGROUND

There are a number of legends that spread suspicion about the unseen places underground. In one rare example, the long rumoured Puebla Tunnels in Mexico were found by contractors in 2015.

Well To Hell
In the 1980s, there were rumours that Russian engineers had drilled to unfathomable depths when they heard the screams of hell itself. An early version of the tale came from American Christian TV network TBN in 1989.

A Norwegian teacher found this amusing and sent the story to Finnish Christian periodical *Vaeltajat* as a prank. The story soon spread as a legend. In 1998, a listener to paranormal radio show *Coast to Coast AM* shared an alleged audio recording from the dig site. The audio sounded much like the antics of an indoor swimming pool.

Enter in Event of Apocalypse
Many urban areas are rumoured to hide secret bunkers. During the Cold War, train enthusiasts speculated the British government had a secret subterranean cache of steam trains for use in a hypothetical post-apocalyptic future.

Subterranean Supercomputer
Students from the University of Illinois once spread rumours that a governmental supercomputer was hidden under the Foreign Language Building. It was also claimed the building's layout was deliberately confusing to deter would-be Soviet invaders in a hypothetical Third World War. The rumours likely started as jokes.

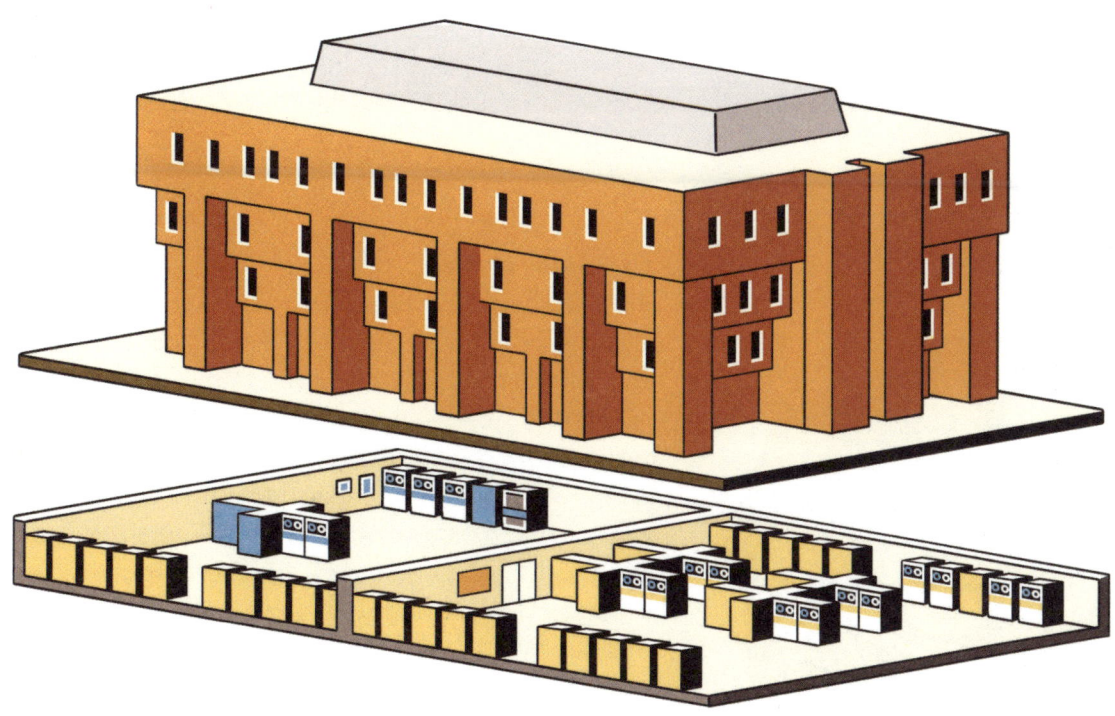

WORK OF THE DEVIL

Many religiously themed urban legends are preoccupied with the fear of Satan. To the most paranoid believers, it appears the Prince of Darkness has influence in even the most mundane products.

Procter & Gamble
Since the 1980s, rumours spread that the Proctor and Gamble logo was evidence of a Satanic pact. Some spread ridiculous misinformation that the P&G president had appeared on TV to declare his profits went to the Church of Satan. P&G later took rival company Amway Corp. to court for encouraging rumours and were awarded $19.25 million in damages.

The Devil's Music
Historically, music has drawn suspicion in those looking for signs of Satan. In the 17th century, England's puritan dictatorship banned what they thought to be lowly music, believing it lead to spiritual corruption. In 1982, a legislative committee gathered in Sacramento, USA to listen to Led Zeppelin played backwards. Assemblyman Phillip Wyman alleged that the music contained praise for Satan and was being used to corrupt the minds (and souls) of the youth. The belief in these hidden hellish messages was widespread with some parent groups like PASS, attempting to block the staging of rock concerts.

It's a Deal

The story goes that during the 1930s, Mississippian Robert Johnson was passionate about becoming a great blues musician. One night, he came upon a crossroads outside the Dockery Plantation (the exact crossroads change with each retelling) where he struck a deal with the Devil to become a skilled musician. In reality, Johnson quickly mastered his craft through hard work and practise.

The legend seems to be inspired by a mixture of Johnson's lyrical reference to the devil and old folklore. Crossroads are one of many symbolic boundaries in folklore. Shrine spirits, gods and Christian saints can still be found marking crossroads to bless travellers. In Hoodoo (an African American magical belief system), it is thought spirits inhabit crossroads, where they may be placated by sacrifice and offerings.

More Celebrity Satan Endorsement

While the moral panic about bands like Led Zeppelin hiding Satanic messages may seem silly in retrospect, similar legends circulate about contemporary acts on a regular basis. Social media is full of people accusing stars like Rihanna, Lady Gaga and Miley Cyrus of being secret Satan worshippers. Evidence, as it was in the past, is typically based on wardrobe choices and the selective interpretation of lyrics.

STRANGE PLACES

Urban legends are sometimes attached to a specific place. They are used to explain an odd feature or characteristic, or in other cases to warn of an invisible paranormal danger.

Plum Island Pink House, Newbury, MA, USA
Supposedly, in the 1920s a divorced man was charged by the court to build a new home for his ex-wife. Out of spite, he chose to build it on lonely marshland. The organisation 'Save the Pink House' discovered little truth to the legend, though the original owners did separate shortly after moving in.

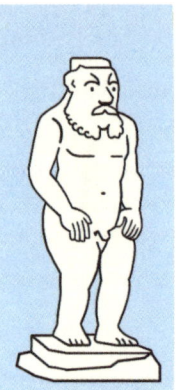 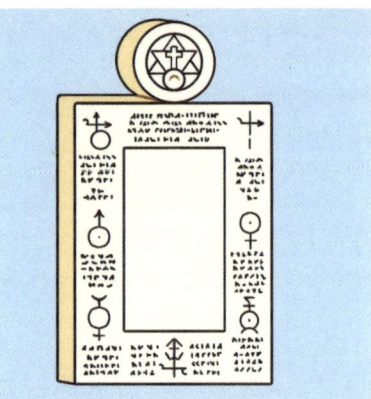

Witches Pond, Bucharest, Romania
According to local legend, this pond has attracted witches since the Middle Ages. Some associate it with Vlad III of Wallachia (the inspiration behind Dracula), as his ghost is thought to haunt the area. Today, legend has become a reality as the spot is visited by practising witches (Wicca) drawn to its legend.

Porta Alchemica, Rome, Italy
Italian for 'alchemy door', this door to nowhere is the remnant of a 17th century villa. A 19th century legend recounted that a famed alchemist once disappeared through the door, leaving only flakes of gold behind them.

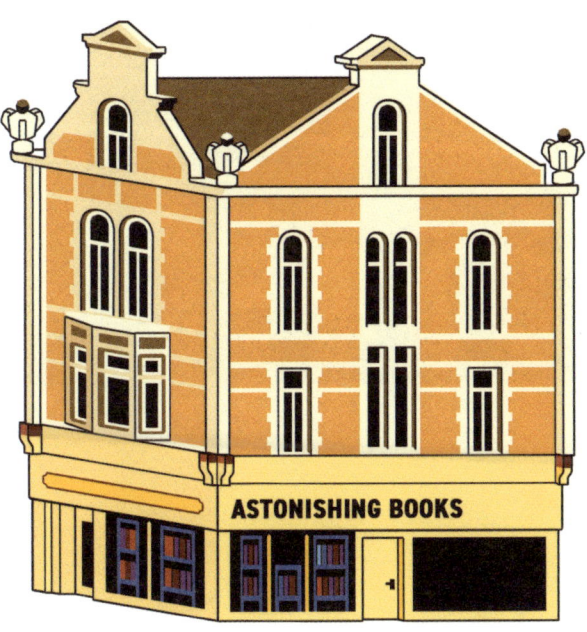

Sorcerer's Apprentice, Leeds, UK
This occult shop opened in 1975 and was one of the first businesses to sell magical ephemera by mail. There were rumours that staff and clientele performed magic rituals in a nearby park, and even summoned a spider monster. In 1989, a moral panic about alleged Satanism led to one of their premises being burned down by Christian fundamentalists.

Choi Hung Station, Hong Kong, China
This train station has a number of unused platforms. According to legend, they were decommissioned after an unusual incident during the station opening in 1979. Apparently, a test train arrived 30 minutes late and its passengers were seen to act oddly. It was thought by some the train had briefly slipped through a portal to hell.

TERRIBLE TECHNOLOGY

One of the more mundane anxieties to feature in urban legends is the fear and confusion with technology. For every gizmo, there is a story about its misuse or unusual abilities.

Cassandra Copier

In the early 2000s, Japanese internet forum users spoke of a convenience store with a magic photocopier. Supposedly, if you put your face in the scanner, it would print a photo of your face on the day of your death. One man was said to have been disappointed with the copier printing a seemingly unchanged, un-aged copy of his face. He was soon killed by a truck after stepping out of the store. The tale was likely made up as a horror story.

Killer Numbers

Some believe in the existence of cursed phone numbers. During the 2000s in Indonesia and Korea, there were tales of calls from strange numbers such as '000-000-000'. The caller was said to ask recipients to carry out a task (like call certain people) or suffer a terrible fate. In the era of smart phones, there is a similar belief in Pakistan about receiving calls from a number illuminated in red.

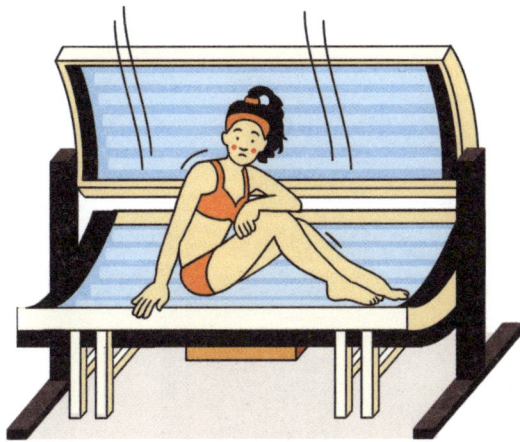

Sunburn

The yarn goes that a tanning salon customer started to feel ill and visited her doctor. The doctor discovered that the patient's internal organs had been slowly cooked by excessive tanning rays. The story is thought to have first circulated in America during the 1980s and relies on the misunderstanding that tanning booths function like microwaves.

Y2K

The Y2K problem was a widespread concern that computers would stop working in the year 2000. Many computer programs used double digits to store dates (i.e. 98), so people thought they would go from 1999 to 1900 and promptly cause catastrophic errors. Fringe groups stoked rumours that the world would be plunged into an apocalypse, leading some people to panic-buy fuel and food. When the day finally came, the bug was relatively small scale and was easily resolved by computer engineers.

OBJECTS OF URBAN LEGENDS

1. Plaster cast of Bigfoot's footprint, CA, USA – Made by Jerry Crew in 1958.
2. Pop Rocks – In legend, a child exploded after consuming a large amount of Pop Rocks and Coca-Cola.
3. Phantom Photocopier, Japan – A legendary photocopier said to predict the death of the user.
4. Flickering Lamppost, Warsaw, Poland – Believed to convey secret messages during the Cold War.
5. Mystery Soda Machine, Seattle, USA – A vending machine that stocked rare drinks until 2018. The machine's owner was a mystery.
6. Crystal Skulls, South America – Quartz skulls allegedly made by Aztec or Maya hundreds of years ago. All are believed to be fakes made mostly by 19th century artefact dealer, Eugène Boban.
7. Ica Stones, Peru – Supposedly pre-Colombian stones that have carvings of dinosaurs and other anachronistic animals. The stones were faked by Peruvian farmer Basilo Uschuya in the 1960s.
8. White BIC Lighter, worldwide – According to legend, several famous musicians had a white lighter in their pocket during their untimely death.
9. Devil's Chair, FL, USA. A cemetery bench – In legend, offerings of unopened beer are said to be drank by the Devil or a ghost.

10. Yeti Scalp, Nepal – Likely a goat hide.
11. Love Lock, worldwide – The tradition of writing the names of loved ones on padlocks is sometimes attributed to a Serbian legend during the First World War.
12. Toynbee Tiles, The Americas – Messages embedded in asphalt by unknown persons in the 1980s. Many legends arose about their meaning and purpose. They were likely made by a conspiracy theorist.
13. Shoe Trees, worldwide – A common act of vandalism around the world. There are a number of urban legends about their meaning.
14. 20202020, UK – Supposedly in the 70s, if one dialled the number in a phone booth they would hear a woman repeating, 'Help me, Susie's dying'.
15. Polybius, USA – A legendary arcade machine supposedly used to brainwash people.
16. Guidestones, GA, USA – Cryptic megaliths built in the 1970s. Local legends claimed they belonged to a secret cult. The guide stones were destroyed by an unknown bomber in 2022.
17. Tamil bell, New Zealand – A bronze bell that belonged to a Māori woman in the 19th century. The extreme age of the bell, and its Tamil inscription, suggest it originated in South Asia, but how it got to New Zealand is a mystery.
18. Musical Chairs Alone, worldwide – A ritual in which one supposedly summons an evil spirit.
19. Shroud of Turin, Italy – Supposedly the death shroud of Jesus of Nazareth. Likely a fake made in the Middle Ages.

METAMODERN ERA

Poster for the film adaptation of a Japanese urban legend, Kisaragi Station, 2022.

VIDEOGAMES

Since their introduction to the general market in the 1970s, video games have inspired many urban legends. Equally, urban legends have inspired the content of video games, including direct references and Easter eggs.

Polybius
The story goes that an arcade game machine in the 1980s, called Polybius, was used to run experiments on players. Maintained by shadowy government types, the machine was said to cause nightmares and hallucinations. The oldest report of the machine was made around the year 2000 on the website coinop.org. Skeptics have suggested the story was made up to attract website visitors.

Nintendo Cartridge (1983)
When game console cartridges fail to work, many players have tried blowing into them. There is little evidence that this works.

Mew, Pokémon Blue & Red (1996)
Players once rumoured that the rare Pokémon 'Mew' could be found hidden under a truck. Developers have hidden items under trucks in later games.

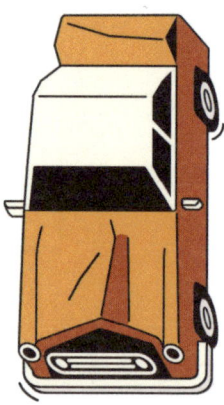

Ghost Car, GTA: San Andreas (2004)
Abandoned cars that spawn in rural areas. The cars sometimes spawn on steep hills, which make them roll downhill when the player arrives.

Grand Theft Auto

Players of *Grand Theft Auto: San Andreas* (2004) once hunted for evidence of Bigfoot (see page 60) in the game's foggy rural areas. Much like with the 'real' Bigfoot, internet forums were flooded with alleged sightings and hoaxed images. The later title *Grand Theft Auto V* (2013) engaged a new batch of theorists with in-game murals and cryptic clues. To this day, Easter egg hunters search the game for evidence of answers to their theories, which in all likelihood will never be answered.

17th Colossus, Shadow of the Colossus (2005)
The game features 16 bosses called colossi. Despite this, players spent years trying locate a final boss that doesn't exist.

Herobrine, Minecraft (2009)
A ghost-like character that has supposedly haunted players since 2010. Developers have added official in-game cosmetics and references to the character.

IKZ, Red Dead Redemption 2 (2018)
Missing posters for the princess Isabeau Katharina Zinsmeister led players to agonise over her location. It was discovered that the content was cut.

SCREEN LEGENDS

Some legends concern speculation about the production and meaning of films.

A Bomb
The Conqueror (1956) stars John Wayne as Genghis Khan in a critically derided epic. Outdoor scenes were filmed downwind of a nuclear test site. Years later, 91 of the 220 crew members developed cancer, leading to rumours that nuclear fallout was the cause.

Shining Moon
The Shining (1980) is a surreal horror film by Stanley Kubrick. Some believe it contains references to Kubrick's alleged role in faking the Moon landing (see page 63). The most blatant reference held up by theorists is the character Danny wearing an Apollo 11 jumper.

Where's my Hoverboard?
Back to the Future Part II (1989) features futuristic inventions such as the hoverboard. Rumours circulated that they were real products of the US toy manufacturing company Mattel but were suppressed due to safety issues. The legend originated from a joke made on a making-of TV special.

Found Footage

The Blair Witch Project (1999) is a found-footage horror film. The film's website helped convince some viewers that the film and its events were real.

Dark Side of the Rainbow

Supposedly, if you play the Pink Floyd album *Dark Side of the Moon* (1973) whilst watching the *Wizard of Oz* (1939), the two are perfectly synchronised. The band members have vehemently denied this is intentional.

This is a True Story

The dark comedy film *Fargo* (1996) begins with a caption asserting that it is based on a true story. In 2001, a Japanese woman was found dead from suicide in the Minnesota snow. Press rumours immediately circulated that the woman had died trying to find the fictional treasure from Fargo. The legend is the subject of the film *Kumiko, the Treasure Hunter* (2014).

SEND IN THE CLOWNS

Clownery is a performance art that dates to the earliest civilisations. Influential horror writers like Stephen King helped subvert their fun-loving craft into a source of terror. Urban legends reflect the disquiet with evil-looking clowns and cast them as the antagonists of several tall tales.

Clown Panic
During 2016, in Greenbay, USA, photos of clowns lurking in dark urban areas became an internet sensation. The images may have been a publicity stunt for a short film. With Halloween around the corner, the timing was perfect for news outlets.

Pranksters mostly used ready-made costumes from online stores.

Killing Joke
Rumours and fake news websites also spread stories about clowns murdering people. Around Halloween, hysteria led around 500 Pennsylvania State University students to march around campus hunting for a non-existent killer clown. News outlets warned of a clown-instigated 'purge' or attack scheduled for Halloween, leading to clown costume bans and armed citizen patrols.

Clown, Ghost or Alien?

In 1973 on the Isle of Wight, UK, two children encountered what they described to be a cross between a clown, an alien and a robot. The 7-foot tall character called itself 'Sam' and claimed not to be human. After further odd communication, the children left and Sam was never seen again. The sighting was reported to British UFO research group BUFORA, who speculated the story was either a case of childish make-believe… or a genuine alien encounter.

Sam's metallic home, according to the children.

FAR-FLUNG TRAVELLERS

On occasion, far-fetched legends grow around alleged time travellers.

John Titor

In 2000, a user on an internet forum for paranormal enthusiasts identified themselves as John Titor, a 'chromonaut' from the year 2036. Titor claimed his mission had taken him to 1976 to find a computer. He claimed he journeyed to the year 2000 to pick up family photos. Titor dazzled users with diagrams and technical language. Skeptics have named a number of supposed hoaxers behind the persona, presumably created for amusement.

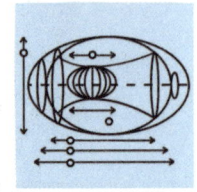

Titor claimed he travelled to the past to locate an IBM model 5110.

Titor's time machine: The General Electric Army Model C204 Gravity Distortion Time Displacement Unit.

Cross-section based on Titor's impressive technical diagrams.

Titor claimed he brought a 1967 Chevrolet to the past for ease of travel.

Time traveller symbol.

SWEET DREAMS

We spend around a third of our lives asleep, so it is no surprise that we have woven a number of urban legends about those unconscious hours and the dreams we conjure.

Watch Your Step
There is a legend that suggests everyone will dream at least once about a village littered with blue bodies. If the dreamer trips and falls, they are said to turn blue and never awake. This legend is known plainly as 'the village where if you fall over, you will die'. The legend originated on Japanese internet forums in the 1990s, and is likely the product of creative writing.

Ever Dream this Man?
According to the story, in 2006, people began to report their dreams were being invaded by an anonymous man with thick eyebrows. The legend was spread through memes and a website created in 2008 by the Italian marketer Andrea Natella. Natella has since said the yarn was a marketing stunt, though what he was trying to sell remains unclear.

Shadow People
Since the early 2000s, internet users have shared stories about shadow people. This legend has been around for as long as insomnia itself and has taken many forms, such as the Hag of European folklore and alien abduction experiences. The phenomena is likely caused by sleep paralysis – when someone is awake but can't move, when in between wakefulness and sleep.

LEGENDARY ROGUES GALLERY

Urban legends are full of colourful villains and the occasional anti-hero. Like ghost stories, they often explore a fear of strangers, and at times, show an archaic discomfort with visible disabilities.

1. Spring-heeled Jack, UK
2. Indrid Cold, USA
3. Bunnyman, USA
4. Slit-mouthed Woman, Japan
5. Phantom Social Worker, UK
6. Man from Taured, Japan
7. Man in Black, USA
8. Woman in Black, USA
9. Black-Eyed Kid, USA
10. Gap Woman, Japan
11. The Hook, USA

12. Dog Lady, USA
13. Phantom Cosmonaut, Space
14. Toucan Man, Costa Rica
15. Killer in the Backseat, worldwide
16. Phantom Hitchhiker, worldwide
17. Resurrection Mary, worldwide
18. John Titor, the future
19. Hammerman, Jordan
20. Eyeless Woman, Korea
21. Dancing Lady, Serbia
22. Aka Manto, Japan
23. Hatman, worldwide
24. Hanako-san, Japan
25. Mary-san, Japan
26. Sadie Farell, USA
27. The Killer Upstairs, USA
28. Pérák, the Springman, Czechia
29. Lift ghost, Philippines
30. Sandbox Woman, Japan
31. Sackman, worldwide

TV DEBUNKERY

Aside from the many television and streaming shows about UFOs, Bigfoot and other cryptids, there have been a few shows to use scientific methods to test the plausibility of more everyday urban legends. None are more influential than the Discovery channel's *Mythbusters* (2003–2016).

1. Jamie Hyneman   2. Adam Savage   3. Kari Byron   4. Tory Belleci   5. Grant Imahara

Mythbusters
Presented by special effects veterans Adam Savage and Jamie Hyneman, Mythbusters used scientific methods to test the probability of urban legends and film stunts. Using Hyneman's workshop and a team of expert staff, the show hinged on the rigging of elaborate experiments. With each experiment, the crew attempted to 'replicate the circumstances, then duplicate the results'. Following which, they assessed whether the tested legend was 'busted', 'plausible' or 'confirmed'. On these pages are a number of the urban legends they tested.

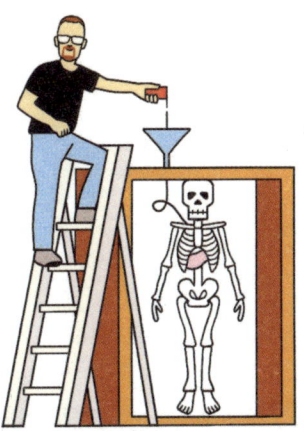

Pop Rocks Explosion (Busted)
An American urban legend in the 1970s suggested that consuming enough Pop Rocks and Coca-Cola could create enough carbon dioxide to make a person explode. In tests, the crew found it only caused considerable discomfort. Do not try at home!

Dynamite Cement Truck (Plausible)
As per an obscure internet legend, the team tested whether dynamite could be used to clean the interior of a cement truck. The team found that using the right amount would indeed fire out shards of solid cement like a canon. Eager for a more impressive explosion, they enlisted the FBI to rig the truck with 850 pounds of blasting agent. The truck did not survive.

JATO Rocket Car (Busted)
In this 1990s legend, one unwise American was said to have died in the manner of a Warner Brothers cartoon having attached a JATO unit (Jet Assisted Take-Off) to his car. The Mythbusters tested the yarn on three occasions and were unable to achieve the speeds or short-lived flight as described in the full tale.

Pane of Glass Decapitation (Plausible)
There is a tale that a motorcyclist was once decapitated by a pane of glass sliding off a truck (as detailed on page 58). The team were able to replicate the result by mounting a pane of glass onto the side of a truck and driving it into a dummy.

INTERNET INVENTION

Since the first forums came online in the 1990s, people have used the internet to share content presented as factual, even if it is a purely creative invention.

Creepypasta

Creepypastas are a subgenre of internet horror content, including stories, pictures, videos and games. The term refers to how short stories were shared on message boards via copy and pasting. Other communities were created in 2010, including the *Creepypasta Wiki* and *r/NoSleep* Reddit forum.

Medieval Found Footage
Lost media encompass videos, text and pictures that are lost to time. An obscure legend tells that one such video showed real footage from medieval Europe (somehow).

Cicada 3301
Between 2012 and 2014, internet puzzles were posted anonymously under the name 3301. People speculated the puzzles were a recruitment tool for the CIA.

Webdriver Torso
From 2014, the Youtube account Webdriver Torso began uploading thousands of peculiar abstract videos. It was revealed to be a test by Google.

Red Room
In the age before pop-up blockers, there were rumours of an unwelcome window with the text 'Do you like the red room?' It was said those who tried to close the window would watch their monitor turn red and be frightened to death. This story was likely inspired by a flash game circulated on a Japanese website during the late 1990s.

Momo, made by Link Factory | Sirenhead, made by Trevor Henderson | The Rake, made by a 4chan user | smile.jpg, made by a 4chan user | Loab, made by Steph Maj Swanson | Kunekune, made by 2channel users

Pantheon of Bogeymen
Much like traditional urban legends, the internet is home to a multitude of creative villains, monsters and bogeymen. In many cases it is simple enough to track down their origins as artworks and creepypasta. It is common for the creator's intent and context to be lost through time and resharing. For example, in 2018, a sculpture made by Japanese company Link Factory was used as the basis for an online hysteria known as the Momo challenge.

Slenderman
Slenderman was a fictional character invented by American writer Eric Knudsen in 2009. The character was depicted as a tall faceless man in black who haunts children. Slenderman quickly became a popular muse of edited photos, video games and movies. Attention was drawn to the character in 2014 due to the stabbing of a 12-year-old American girl, who thankfully survived. The assailants, two girls of a similar age, claimed they carried out the attack to appease Slenderman. It was soon found one of the assailants was mentally ill. Those in the creepypasta community rallied to raise money for the victim. Much media debate ensued, following the familiar rhetoric of whether books, films and videos games lead to children being violent.

RITUALS

Some urban legends take the form of a list of instructions or ritual. If followed correctly they promise either pleasant or horrifying results.

Elevator Game
In this game, the participant is encouraged to follow a strict list of instructions in a lift. If done correctly, it is said the participant can find another world. The strange world is typically described as being unremarkable besides being dark and scary. The legend suggests that if the directions are followed incorrectly, the participant will become lost forever. This ritual was popularised in the 2010s on Korean social media, but may have originated years prior on the website 2ch.

Kaijin Answer
Using mobile phones, ten players in a circle call the person to their right. Once all phones are busy it is said the ghost, Kaijin, will answer. Kaijin will allow nine of the people to ask any question (for instance, asking for lottery numbers). Kaijin will then ask the tenth person an impossible question. When they inevitably fail to answer, a pale hand will emerge from their phone screen and attack! This legend has circled the internet in Japan since the 2000s. It is believed the story was made up by a horror writer.

The Midnight Man

Illuminated only by candles at before midnight, a lone player is instructed to follow a complicated ritual to summon a ghostly entity called the Midnight Man. The objective is to avoid meeting the Midnight Man who is presumably very frightening. This particular ritual has been in circulation since the mid 2010s, but bears resemblance to a 19th century séance (a traditional method for talking to ghosts).

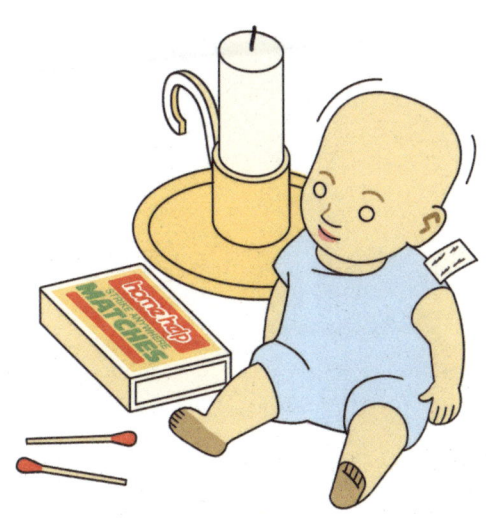

Some of the objects needed for an infamous Japanese ritual game called 'Hide and Seek Alone'.

PHANTOM PLACES

Some contemporary urban legends concern the existence or non existence of towns and cities. Their uncertain nature is the subject of fantastical and humorous tales.

Sugisawa Village
It is said the forests of Japan conceal the ruined Sugisawa Village, haunted by villagers murdered in the 1920s. Since the mid-2000s posters on Japanese websites shared their alleged encounters with the accursed village. The posters told of creepy laughter and rooms packed with angry ghosts.

This tale was likely inspired by a very real, tragic mass murder in 1928, taking place in Kano, Okayama Prefecture. Fictional aspects of the urban legend were probably inspired by highly influential video games like *Silent Hill* (1999).

Invisible City of Biringan

Somewhere in the Province of Samar in the Philippines there supposedly dwells the hidden city of Biringan. Sailors claim to have caught glimpses of its lights on moonless nights. People deemed suitable for its population are spirited away by its *engkantos* inhabitants, from the Spanish word *encanto*, meaning enchantment. Those who wander into Biringan accidentally are warned not to eat any food they find, or else they will be trapped there.

This story has been in circulation since the 1960s, with the earliest internet reference dating to around 2007. It is similar to other folkloric legends of spirit and fairy kingdoms, such as the Magonia in France.

Bielefeld Does Not Exist

In the late 1990s, German internet users spread a satirical conspiracy that the city of Bielefeld didn't exist and was made up by a group known as *SIE* (German for *THEM*). Similarly, in the mid 2010s, an American internet user spread a joke rumour that Finland didn't exist. To their surprise, the conspiracy gained seemingly earnest supporters. This is an example of 'Poe's Law' – in which satire can be mistaken as sincere when the author's intent isn't clear.

URBAN LEGENDS IN MEDIA

Urban legend have made many appearances in books, films, TV and video games. Some of these urban legends are invented by writers to serve as plot devices, villains and world building.

1. The Springman, *Pérák a SS* (1946)
2. Hitchhikers, *Return to Glennascaul* (1951)
3. Fouke Monster, *The Legend of Boggy Creek* (1972)
4. Bigfoot, *Harry and the Hendersons* (1987)
5. Jersey Devil, *The X-Files* (1993)
6. Nessie, *Loch Ness* (1996)
7. Mothman, *The Mothman Prophecies* (2002)
8. Pig, *Tales from the Golden Age* (2009)
9. Stree, *Stree* (2018)
10. Elvis, *Good Omens* (2019)
11. The Bridge Curse (2020)
12. Strange Lady, *Juju Stories* (2021)

CRYPTID PHOTOS

In lieu of good specimens to study, the most provocative evidence for cryptids are the alleged photos and films showing their activity or decayed remains. Like pictures of UFOs and ghosts, most examples are blurry and indistinct.

1.

2.

3.

4.

5.

6.

7.

1. 'Bigfoot', USA, 1967
Known as the Patterson–Gimlin film. Skeptics believe that the footage depicts a man in a suit.

2. 'Sea Monster', New Zealand, 1977
Known as the Zuiyo-Maru Carcass. This odd discovery was later identified as the remains of a basking shark.

3. 'Nessie', UK, 1977
A photo taken by artist and performer Tony Shiels. Skeptics believe the photo was a hoax.

4. Queen of Sheba's Gazelle, Qatar, 1985
Thought to have been extinct since they were last seen in Yemen in 1951. In 1985 a photo surfaced which seemingly showed a number of the gazelles in a private Qatari zoo.

5. 'Wolf', Japan, 1996
Wolves are thought to have been extinct in Japan, ever since 1905. Mountaineer, Hiroshi Yaji, took exceptionally clear pictures of a wolf-like animal he saw in the road. Some believe they simply show a feral dog.

6. 'Skunkape', USA, 2000
One of two pictures seemingly taken within seconds of each other by an anonymous photographer. Skeptics believe it was either a clever collage or simply a person in a suit.

7. Fresno Nightcrawlers, USA, 2007
Alleged security camera footage showing white trouser-like creatures walking across the frame. It was most likely achieved with clever puppetry.

URBAN LEGENDS TODAY

Urban legends continue to travel under the guise of fake news, social media posts and in the traditional context of local gossip. It is common to pass on stories uncritically, without interrogating their truth or possible meaning. People enjoy good stories with archetypes, dramatic payoffs and punchlines. Stories are progressively embroidered, making them pan-generational quilts of horror and humour.

Authors from previous decades bemoaned the dying art of urban legends with the rise of digital literacy. But the digital age has only allowed people to convey the same old legends in a new way. Bogeymen, misconceptions, jokes and parabolic yarns play on with new masks.

I hope this book has helped you to consider the urban legends known to you. They are as fluid as time, ceaselessly picking up and discarding context and content to fit the moment.

Pertinently, they remind us to ask the import question:

Have you checked the under the bed?

(REAL) PEOPLE OF URBAN LEGENDS

1. Jacob Grimm, folklorist
2. Wilhelm Grimm, folklorist
3. Rosebud Yellow Robe, folklorist
4. Tom Slick, Yeti Hunter
5. Ivan T. Sanderson, cryptozoologist
6. Kunio Yanagita, scholar, folklorist
7. Bernard Heuvelmans, cryptozoologist
8. Teodoro Vidal, folklorist
9. Charles Fort, author
10. Gray Barker, writer
11. Arthur C. Clarke, writer
12. John Keel, writer
13. Jon-Erik Beckjord, paranormal researcher
14. Gillian Bennett, folklorist
15. Richard M. Dorson, folklorist
16. J. Allen Hynek, ufologist
17. Iikura Yoshiyuki, scholar
18. Jan Harold Brunvand, writer
19. Colin Bord, folklorist
20. Janet Bord, folklorist
21. James Ogude, folklorist
22. Roger Patterson, bigfooter
23. Aurelio M. Espinosa, folklorist
24. Loren Coleman, cryptozoologist
25. Linda Dégh, folklorist
26. Linda Godfrey, writer
27. Kathryn Lawson Morgan, folklorist
28. Lucia Peters, writer

29. Bob Gimlin, bigfooter
30. David Clarke, writer, journalist
31. Art Bell, radio host
32. Todd Lawrence, folklorist
33. Arthur Goldstuck, writer
34. David Mikkelson, Snopes founder
35. Heather Joseph Witham, folklorist
36. Matt Moneymaker, presenter
37. Patricia Turner, folklorist
38. Ranae Holland, presenter, skeptic
39. Jamie Hyneman, presenter
40. Adam Savage, presenter
41. Grant Imahara, engineer, presenter
42. Kari Byron, presenter
43. Tory Belleci, presenter
44. Annie Barrows, writer
45. Barbara Mikelson, Snopes founder
46. Tara A. Devlin, writer
47. Deborah Hyde, skeptic, folklorist
48. Travis Taylor, scientist, presenter
49. Lamont Pearley, folklorist
50. Ben Hanson, presenter
51. Claudia Ackley, bigfooter
52. Phillis May Machunda, folklorist
53. Josh Gates, presenter
54. Jeremy Wade, survivalist, presenter
55. Johnathan Frakes, presenter
56. Hayley Stevens, skeptic, writer
57. Marcus Parks, podcaster
58. Ben Kissel, podcaster
59. Henry Zabrowski, podcaster
60. Chris Carter, X-Files creator
61. Jon Y. Lee, folklorist
62. William Hawthorn Wiggins Jr, folklorist
63. Les Stroud, presenter
64. Aaron Mahnke, writer
65. James 'Bobo' Fay, presenter
66. David Emery, editor

GLOSSARY

Apotropaic magic
Supposed protective magical measures against evil and monsters.

Bogeyman
A mythic and legendary figure used by parents to frighten children into good behaviour.

Creepypasta
Internet-circulated horror fiction often presented as true.

Conspiracy theory
The belief that there is a secret plan by a group of people.

Cryptid
An animal whose existence is unsubstantiated.

Cryptozoology
The study of legendary animals whose existence is in dispute.

Chain-letter
A letter, message or email that is written to convince the recipient to spread it further.

Flap
The high volume of sightings of an unexplained phenomenon, typically over a short period of time.

Folklore
Stories and beliefs passed through oral tradition.

FOAF
The reference to a 'friend of a friend' is often used to give credibility to an urban legend.

Globster
An unidentified organic mass washed up on the shore. Decomposed sharks are often misidentified as sea monsters.

Haunting
An area, person or object associated with frequent or repeated paranormal activity.

High strangeness
A term coined by ufologist J. Allen Hynek, referring to peculiar details from UFO cases, often applied to other areas of the paranormal.

Mass hysteria
A group panic based on fear, sometimes causing collective illusions and odd behaviour.

Memetic hazard
A term from horror fiction; urban legends sometimes reference ideas or images that can kill.

Legend-tripping
A rite-of-passage in which adolescents visit somewhere with a legendary reputation.

Occult
The broad study of magic, mysticism and the paranormal.

Ostension
Folklorists use this word to describe how real-life events can imitate a legend.

Pareidolia
Finding patterns in random data – for example, a face on toast.

Pseudo-ostension
When people behave in a certain way because they believe in a legend.

Poe's law
The adage that without a clear authorial intent, satire can be mistaken as sincere.

Scarelore
Tales shared with the intention of frightening the audience.

Skeptic
An individual who values scientific inquiry and methodology.

Sleep paralysis
An experience in which people awake unable to move. Often accompanied with hallucinations and the feeling of being weighed down.

Urban legends
Typically, humorous and horrific stories circulated as true. In most instances, they are invention or exaggeration.

Woo
The use of scientific-sounding words to support fringe theory, and a sound ghosts make.

Xeroxlore
Urban legends spread through fliers and posters.

FURTHER READING

COLBY, C. B., (1959) *Strangely Enough*, Reprint, Scholastic Book Services, 1963, USA

VALLÉE, Jacques, (1969) *Passport to Magonia*, Reprint, Daily Grail Publishing, 2014, Brisbane, Australia

HYNEK, J. Allen, *The UFO Experience: A Scientific Inquiry*, Abelard & Schuman Ltd, 1972, London, UK

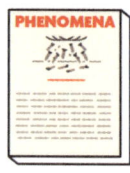
MICHELL, John & RICKARD, Robert, *Phenomena*, Thames and Hudson Ltd, 1977, London, UK

WILDING-WHITE, Ted, *The World of the Unknown: UFOs*, Usborne Publishing Ltd, 1977, Burlington, Canada

MAYNARD, Christopher, (1977), *The World of the Unknown: Ghosts*, Reprint, Usborne Publishing Ltd, 2019, London, UK

BRUNVAND, Jan Harold (1984), *The Chocking Doberman*, Reprint, Penguin Books, 1987, London, UK

SLEMAN, Thomas, *Strange But True*, London Bridge, 1998, London, UK

BRUNVAND, Jan Harold, *Too Good to Be True: Urban Legends*, Norton & Company Inc, 1999, New York, USA

CRAUGHWELL, Thomas J., (1999) *Urban Legends*, Reprint, Black Dog & Leventhal Publishers Inc, 2005, New York, USA

DANIELEWSKI, Mark Z., *House of Leaves*, Pantheon Books, 2000 New York, USA

BRUNVAND, Jan Harold, *Encyclopaedia of Urban Legends*, Reprint, ABC-CLIO, 2001, Santa Barbara, USA

FIERY, Ann, *The Completely and Totally True Book of Urban Legends*, Running Press, 2001, Philadelphia, USA

CLARKE, Roger, *A Natural History of Ghosts: 500 Years of Hunting for Proof*, Reprint, Penguin Books Ltd, 2012, London UK

 LOXTON, Daniel & PROTHERO, Donald R., *Abominable Science!*, Colombia University Press, 2012, New York, USA

 RUICKBIE, Leo, *Ghost Hunting*, Constable & Robinson Ltd, 2013, London, UK

 WOMACK, Jack, *Flying Saucers are Real!*, Anthology Editions, 2016, New York, USA

 MAHNKE, Aaron, *The World of Lore: Monstrous Creatures*, Del Trey, 2017, New York, USA

 DEVLIN, Tara A., *Toshiden Vol. 1*, Oroshi Press, 2018, USA

 JIMÉNEZ, RAÚL, *Myths and Urban Legends: Mexico*, Self-Published, 2022, Mexico

 SHAW, Martin, *Unexplained Scotland*, Peregrine Press, 2022, UK

 SCHREIBER, Dan, *The Theory of Everything Else*, Harper Collins 2022, London, UK

FURTHER VIEWING

It should go without saying that most films and TV series that feature urban legends are in the horror genre. Only watch if you are old and brave enough!

 *The Haunting,* [Film] Robert Wise, 1963

 *Unsolved Mysteries,* [TV] John Cosgrove, Terry Dunn Meuer, 1987

 *Scooby Doo, Where Are You?,* [TV] Joe Ruby & Ken Spears, 1969

 *Candyman,* [Film] Bernard Rose, 1992

 *The Legend of Boggy Creek,* [Film], Charles B. Pierce, 1972

 *The X-Files,* [TV] Chris Carter, 1993

 *The Wickerman,* [Film] Robin Hardy, 1973

 *Scream,* [Film] Wes Craven, 1996

 *Black Christmas,* [Film] Bob Clark, 1974

 *I Know What You Did Last Summer,* [Film] Jim Gillespie, 1997

 *Close Encounters of a Third Kind,* [Film] Stephen Spielberg, 1977

 *Buffy the Vampire Slayer,* [TV] Joss Whedon, 1997

 *Harry and the Hendersons,* [Film] William Dear, 1987

 *Beyond Belief: Fact or Fiction,* [TV] Lynn Lehmann, 1997

 *Ringu*, [Film] Hideo Nakata, 1998

 *Urban Legend*, [Film] Jamie Blanks, 1998

 *The Blair Witch Project*, [Film] Daniel Myrick, 1999

 *The Mothman Prophecies*, [Film] Mark Pellington, 2002

 *Mythbusters*, [TV] Peter Rees, 2003

 *50 States of Fright*, [TV], Sam Raimi, et al, 2013

 *The Vast of Night*, [Film] Andrew Patterson, 2019

 *The Empty Man*, [Film] David Prior, 2020

INDEX

A
abominable snowman 48-9
Adomnán 18
aircraft 40-1, 43
Aka Manto 79
aliens 64, 99, 101
alligators 83
animals 11-12, 18-21, 28, 46-7, 82-3
Antarctic 39
apocalypse 85, 91
artefacts, weird 58
astronauts 64-5
Aswang 27
Atlantis 24
attractions, accursed 54-5
Australia 20, 30, 34, 77

B
Back to the Future Part II 96
Barker, Gray 67
barometer question 77
barrel of bricks tale 76
Beardsley, Richard 51
bears 46-7
The Beatles 57
Beck, Reynard 66
bedsheet ghost 28
Belleci, Tory 104
Benzaiten 54
Betsileo people 26
bibles 36
Bielefeld 111
Bigfoot 62-3, 74, 95, 112
Biringan 111
The Blair Witch Project 97
Bloody Mary 28
bogeymen 11, 107
Bondeson, Jan 72
Bosworth, Brian 76
Britain 31, 35-6, 41, 56, 89
Bubble Yum 73
bunkers, secret 85
Bunnyman 78, 102
Burns, John W. 62
Byrd, Richard E. 39

C
cacti 73
Cadillac, rattle in the 76
the caller 70

Carter brothers 27
cattle mutilation 58
celebrities 56-7, 87
Chadda Group 71
chain letters 81
chewing gum 73
China 29, 48-9, 89
Choi Hung Station 89
CIA 106
cities, lost 24-5
Clootie trees 37
clownery 98-9
Coast to Coast AM 15
Coca Cola 72
coelacanth 21
computers 85, 91, 100
con rit 19
Conley, Brian A. 78
The Conqueror 96
contamination 11, 72-3
cookie recipe 80
Cooper, D. B. 43
cosmonauts, phantom 64, 102
creepypasta 106-7
Crew, Jerry 62
crossroads 87
cryptids 47, 49, 74-5
cryptozoology 12, 46-7

D
Dahut 25
The Daily Mail 49
Death Valley stones 59
decapitation 60, 104
the Devil 86-7, 89
dinosaurs 21
disappearances, mysterious 42-3
Disney, Walt 56
Disneyland, ghosts of 54
dodo 21
Dog Lady 23, 102
dogs 22-3, 82
Dorson, Richard 10
Doyle, Arthur Conan 20
Dracula 26
dragged roofer tale 76
dreams 101
dresses, poisoned 72
Due, Dearg 27

duppy 28
dynamite cement truck 105

E
Earhart, Amelia 42
Edison, Thomas 42
El Dorado 24
Empusa 27
eyebrow man 101

F
fan deaths 60
Fargo 97
fast food 73
fatalities, freaky 60-1
Fazilpur Badli 59
films 96-7
Finland 111
firefighters 61
fog 38
folklorists 12, 14
Foo Fighters 40

G
gang initiation 81
gap woman 71, 102
Gardner, Robert Coe 41
ghosts 12, 15, 28-9, 34, 54, 60, 108-9
Gideons 36
Gimlet, Bob 63
globsters 19
Grand Theft Auto 94-5
grandma, runaway 9
Greece 27, 37, 39, 72
greetings cards 81
gremlins 41
Grimm, Brothers 14

H
hairdos, horrid 60
Halloween 78, 98
hamsters 83
Hankey, Rosalie 51
Hell 84
Hendrix, Jimi 56
Heracles 72
Heuvelmans, Bernard 47
Himalayas 48-9
hitchhiker, phantom 51, 103
hoaxers, ghost 34

hollow Earth conspiracy 39
hollow-eyed woman 79
Holt, Harold 42
home invaders 70-1
Hoodoo practises 87
the hook 50, 102
hotel legends 36
hoverboards 96
humming, phantom 59
humorous legends 76-7
Hyneman, Jamie 104

I
ice 59
Indonesia 55, 91
Inokashira Park 54
internet inventions 106-7
Isle of Wight 99

J
Japan 23, 28, 54, 71, 77, 79, 90, 101, 110
jean-clad bather 104
Jinmenken 23
Johnson, Robert 87
Jorge, Don 27

K
Kaijin 108
kangaroo thief 77
Keel, John 67
KFC 73
Knudsen, Eric 107
Komodo dragon 46
Krahang 66
Kubrick, Stanley 96

L
La Santa Compaña 28
Le Prince, Louis 42
Led Zeppelin 86-7
Lemuria 25
the licked hand 71
lifts 29, 103, 108
lighthouses 38
lights, little 30-1
Lizard people 39
Loch Ness Monster 18-9, 74
Loys, François de 46
Luces del Tesoro 31
Luz da Caniceira 30

M

Machu Picchu 24
Mad Gasser 35
Malay cultures 26
Mars 64
McCartney, Paul 57
media legends 56-7
medieval footage 106
Men in Black 79, 102
mice 72
Michael, George 56
microwaves 82
Midnight Man 109
Min Min lights 30
Minecraft 95
moa 21
Momo challenge 107
Mongolia 48
monkeys 46
the Moon 64-5, 96
Mothman 66-7, 75
motorcyclists 60
mummies 38
Mum's the word 36
Murray, Douglas 38
music 86-7
Mythbusters 104-5

N

Nandi bear 46-7, 75
NASA 65
Natella, Andrea 101
Newman, Henry 48
Nintendo 94

O

objects 112-13
okapi 46
oral traditions 14
organ thieves 36
ostension 15

P

Pakistan 71, 91
parakeets 56
Patterson, Roger 63
Penanggalan 26
Pennsylvania State University 98
pens, space 65
people of urban legends, real 116-17
Pérák the Springman 41, 103
Phantom Motorcyclist of Elmore 60
phenomena 58-9
phone numbers, cursed 91
photocopier, phantom 90, 112
Pink Floyd 97
places: phantom 110-11
  strange 88-9
Plato 24
Plum Island Pink House 88
Poe's Law 111
Pokémon 94
poltergeists 28
Polybius 94
Pop Rocks 105, 112
Porta Alchemica 88
prehistoric animals 20-1
Presley, Elvis 57
procoptodon 20
Procter & Gamble 80, 86
pseudo-ostension 15
psychological warfare 27

R

Ramanga 26
rats 73
Red Dead Redemption 95
red room 107
rituals 108-9
road rumours 11, 50-1
Roe, William 62
rogues, legendary 102-3
Roswell Incident 53
Russia 64-5, 84

S

sabre-toothed tiger 21
salacious sprees 34-5
'Sam' 99
Sanderson, Ivan T. 20
Sasquatch 62
Satanic symbols 80, 86
Savage, Adam 104
scuba divers 61
sea legends 38
Second World War 40-1
Semczuk, Przemysław 51
Serbian dancing lady 79, 103
sewers 83
Shadow of Colossus 95
shadow people 101
The Shining 96
ships 38
Shipton, Eric 49
Shufelt, George Warren 39
Siegmeister, Walter 39
skeptical enquiry 12-13
Slenderman 107
Slick, Tom 49
social media 15, 87
Sorcerer's Apprentice 89
South Korea 60, 79, 91, 108
space stories 64-5
spiders 73
spontaneous human combustion 58
Spring-Heeled Jack 33, 35, 102
Stead, William 38
Stoker, Bram 26
the stranger 29, 78-9
Strickler, Lon 21
Stubbe, Peter 23
Sugisawa village 110
Sukima-onna 71
sunburn 91

T

Taman Festival Park 55
taxi drivers 29
technology 11, 90-1
Teketeke 79
teleportation 58
Telets, Svetlana 58
thylacines 20
Titor, John 100, 103
toilets 77, 79
trains 85, 89
travellers, far-flung 100
trees 37
TV debunker 104-5

U

UFOs 15, 40, 52-3, 79
underground legends 84-5
underworlds 39
University of Illinois 85
urban legends: skeptical inquiry 12-13
  spread of 14-15
  what they are 10-11

USA 23, 27, 29, 35-7, 39, 51, 53-4, 58-9, 62-3, 66-7, 78, 83, 85, 88, 98

V

vampires 26-7
videogames 94-5
Vietnamese mouse-deer 20
the Village where if you fall over, you will die 101
vishap 19
Vlad III 26, 88
Volga cars 51

W

Wallace, Raymond 62
wartime legends 40-1
Webdriver Torso 106
Weekly World News 57, 64, 76
werewolves 23
white lady 28
Will o'the Wisps 31
wish tree 37
Witches Pond 88
Wizard Bombardier 34
Wyman, Phillip 86

X

xeroxlore 14, 80-1

Y

Y2K 91
Yeren 48
Yeti 47, 48-9, 62, 75, 113
Ys 25
yūrei 28